THE
INCLUSIVE-
LANGUAGE
DEBATE

"Don Carson has given us a much-needed book that is both provocative and timely. . . . He observes that inclusive-language translations are not only inevitable but also necessary, and that current translations that refuse to update themselves gender-inclusively will quite likely end up in the dustbin of history. . . . I heartily and enthusiastically recommend Carson's latest effort, and I do so without reservation."

Ronald Youngblood
member of NIV Committee on Bible Translation

"Carson's study of inclusive language is an excellent plea for sanity in a discussion that has had its share of hysteria and lack of balance. Bringing the history of translation, exegetical skill, an awareness of how different languages work, an appreciation of the cultural dimensions of the question, numerous specific examples, and just sheer calm to the table, Carson's work deserves a careful reading by all in the debate and a hearty word of thanks from the Christian community."

Darrell L. Bock
research professor of New Testament studies,
Dallas Theological Seminary

"Wise and scholarly, D. A. Carson brings judicious insight to the heated debate regarding inclusive language in Bible translations. This profound volume demonstrates the complexity of translation decisions and heightens sensitivity to the task of careful Biblical interpretation."

Luder G. Whitlock, Jr.
president, Reformed Theological Seminary

"Based on masterful linguistic scholarship, this book is a model of fair-minded wisdom on Bible translation."

J. I. Packer
professor of theology, Regent College

"From a surprising source comes an able defense for inclusive language, because of a desire to have integrity in Bible translation."

Aída Besançon Spencer
professor of New Testament
Gordon-Conwell Theological Seminary

THE
INCLUSIVE-
LANGUAGE
DEBATE

A PLEA FOR REALISM

D. A. CARSON

Baker Books
A Division of Baker Book House Co
Grand Rapids, Michigan 49516

© 1998 by D. A. Carson

Published by Baker Books
a division of Baker Book House Company
P.O. Box 6287, Grand Rapids, MI 49516-6287

and

Inter-Varsity Press
38 De Montford Street
Leicester LE1 7GP
England

Printed in the United States of America

Library of Congress Cataloging-in-Publication Data

Carson, D. A.
    The inclusive-language debate : a plea for realism / D.A. Carson.
        p.   cm.
    Includes bibliographical references and indexes.
    ISBN 0-8010-5835-X (pbk.)
        1. Bible—Translating. 2. Nonsexist language—Religious aspects—Christianity. 3. Bible. English—Versions. I. Title.
    BS449.C37   1998
    220.5'2001—dc21   98-23473

British Library Cataloguing in Publication Data
A catalogue record for this book is available from the British Library.
ISBN 0-85111-584-5

For information about academic books, resources for Christian leaders, and all new releases available from Baker Book House, visit our web site:
http://www.bakerbooks.com

This book is gratefully dedicated
to the many Bible translators I have known
and sometimes had the privilege of working with
in places as varied as
Nairobi, Philadelphia, and Ukarumpa

CONTENTS

PREFACE

Let me be frank: this is not the sort of book I like to write. By inclination there are other things I would much rather do. Moreover, experience has taught me that sometimes the effort to pour oil on boiling waters, far from calming the heavy seas, ends up with a conflagration: various parties can hardly wait to touch a match to the oil.

Still, on balance it seemed better to say something than to say nothing. I was exposed to the challenges of translation from my earliest days: I was born in Montréal and reared in French Canada. My father was pastor of a bilingual church, and all of us grew up with both English and French. Of my first two experiences as a pastoral intern, one was in a French church, the other in an English church; of my first two attempts at church planting, one was in an English-speaking suburb, the other in a French-speaking city. I grew up memorizing the King James Version in English and the Louis Segond in French.

Later on I learned other languages, but those early experiences of ministry convinced me of one thing. This was at a time when my knowledge of the biblical languages was still rudimentary, so I was largely dependent on the English and French versions. I discovered that sometimes a sermon I prepared for an English congregation, grounded in the English text, could not easily be preached in French, and vice versa—

unless I spent quite a bit of time trying to explain how the two versions had handled the underlying Greek and Hebrew in rather different ways. From the preacher's perspective, it struck me that if too much of my emphasis depended on peculiarities of translations, I was probably in danger of missing the forest for the trees. So from then on I tried to produce sermons that so focused on what was clear in *both* translations that I could preach them in either language.

Several decades and languages later, I still think that was a good choice at the time. It is not that careful study cannot properly evaluate translations or offer a reasoned judgment as to which one is better, for what audience, and why. But the simple resolution I adopted as a young man did help me to focus at the time on what was central, and I have never regretted the decision.

In the current debate over inclusive language, all sides have raised important and delicate issues. Part of my task in this little book is to utter a plea for realism—to try to make clear, from my perspective, what we can and cannot expect from translations, and how easy it is to miss some of the big issues while focusing on the narrower and more technical ones.

This book is not for experts: linguists will learn nothing from it, and Bible translators very little. As is frequently the case, some of the most strident voices have been raised, on all sides, by concerned Christians who know little of the challenges of translation, and still less of linguistic theory. I have tried to write for people with little or no Greek and Hebrew. Undoubtedly I have been too reductionistic at points and unwittingly too technical at others. Still, if this book fosters among Christians careful, clearheaded discussion about this subject, I shall be grateful.

Four final remarks:

First, for the record, I write as a confessional evangelical with a high view of Holy Scripture and have frequently contributed to conferences and books on the subject.

Second, in the debate between "egalitarians" and "complementarians" I side with the latter, and have sometimes addressed such questions publicly, both orally and in written form.[1] In other words, whatever my errors and blind spots, I cannot fairly be accused of adopting the stances I do in translation because I am driven by some feminist agenda or other. At the same time, I naturally wish not to adopt a position inconsistent with my larger theological convictions in this respect.

Third, this little book does not properly address the serious critique offered by the more radical feminists, who because God is not properly "male" in any sexual or human sense, think that the ancient language of trinitarian confessionalism should be changed from "Father, Son, and Holy Spirit" to "Creator, Child (or Redeemer), and Sustainer" or the like. The questions they raise are important, increasingly sophisticated, and deserve serious evaluation and response. I venture a few remarks here and there. But by and large this book restricts itself to an in-house discussion within the framework of evangelicalism.

Finally, I want to record my thanks to several people who steered me toward important resources. Professor John Stek sent me some of his unpublished papers, and they proved to be brimful of salient observations. Dr. Norman Fraser not only e-mailed me some useful notes on gender systems in various languages around the world but provided me with bibliography that anchored me in some serious research on such matters. Dr. Richard Schultz sent me tapes and notes of the public Wheaton College forum, "The Current Inclusive Language Controversy." My colleagues Drs. Wayne Grudem and Grant Osborne have already gone public with their views on this debate: I have benefited from their work, even though neither will agree with everything I say. Several colleagues took the time to read the first draft of this book and offer helpful criticisms. To each of them I owe a considerable debt. I am grateful for their time and effort.

Soli Deo gloria.

ABBREVIATIONS

ASV	American Standard Version
CBMW	Council on Biblical Manhood and Womanhood
CBT	Committee on Bible Translation
CEV	Contemporary English Version
CS	Colorado Springs
CSG	Colorado Springs Guidelines
IBS	International Bible Society
JB	Jerusalem Bible
KJV	King James Version
LB	Living Bible
LXX	Septuagint (ancient Greek translation of the Old Testament)
MT	Masoretic Text (Hebrew Old Testament)
NASB	New American Standard Bible
NEB	New English Bible
NET	New English Translation
NIrV	New International Reader's Version
NIV	New International Version
NIVI	New International Version: Inclusive Language Edition
NJB	New Jerusalem Bible
NKJV	New King James Version
NLT	New Living Translation
NRSV	New Revised Standard Version
REB	Revised English Bible
RSV	Revised Standard Version

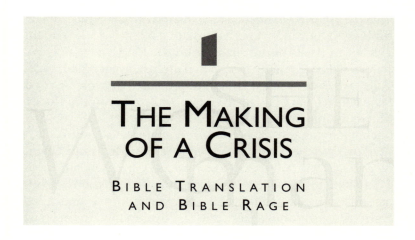

THE MAKING
OF A CRISIS

BIBLE TRANSLATION
AND BIBLE RAGE

Bible Rage

During the past decade or so, traffic experts have coined a new expression: "road rage." People drive thousands of miles, face the ordinary stress of interstate highways, bottlenecks, gapers' blocks, and rush hours. Then someone cuts them off—something that has happened to them scores of times before, something they've probably done themselves more than once—and somehow they go over the top: this incident is personal. Road rage triumphs, and out comes a crowbar or a shotgun, and mayhem is the result.

Bible translation has been going on since at least the second century before Christ, and probably earlier. Normally it is a highly varied but reasonably predictable business. Every once

15

in a while, however, and for highly disparate reasons, Bible rage takes over. In the days of William Tyndale, the issue was translating into the vernacular, into the common language of the people. The Roman Catholic Church was not against all translations, since after all it used the Latin Vulgate. But it was fiercely opposed to vernacular versions (a "version" of the Bible is nothing more than a translation of the Bible). William Tyndale paid with his life: he was strangled and burned in 1536.

It would be tedious to rehearse all the instances of Bible rage. Today we live in relatively mellower times. When the Revised Standard Version (RSV) appeared in 1952, one pastor in Rocky Mount, North Carolina, publicly burned a copy with a blow-torch, damning it as "a heretical, communist-inspired Bible." The ashes were sent in a metal box to Dean Weigle, at Yale Divinity School, who had served as convener of the Standard Bible Committee, responsible for the translation. That box and its ashes are still among the archives of the committee—"a reminder," as Bruce Metzger whimsically puts it, "that, though in previous centuries Bible translators were sometimes burned, today happily it is only a copy of the translation that meets such a fate."[1]

The current debate has fired up various degrees of Bible rage once again. I have not yet heard of a copy of the New International Version: Inclusive Language Edition (NIVI) being scorched with a blowtorch, but the vice president of the International Bible Society (IBS), which sponsors the NIV and the NIVI, has publicly displayed seven copies sent him that had apparently been treated to the tender mercies of a power drill. The controversy has prompted one conservative institution to sack from its faculty a member of the Committee on Bible Translation (CBT—the group responsible for both the NIV and the NIVI) only a year or so before his retirement.[2]

Definitions

But we need to back up a little. By "inclusive-language translations" or "gender-neutral translations" or "gender-inclusive translations" I am referring to English translations of the Bible, or parts of the Bible, that replace male nouns like "man" and "brother" and male pronouns like "he" and "him" with other expressions that clearly include women—hence *inclusive* language. "Man" might become "person," "brother" might become "brother and sister," and so forth. English has its share of both gender-exclusive, or gender-specific, terms (for example, husband, wife, she, father) and gender-inclusive, or gender-neutral, terms (for example, spouse, parent, them, sibling, child). Such expressions are not to be confused with expressions that somehow suggest a blending of terms (for example, unisex, androgynous).

If, then, the donor language, Hebrew or Aramaic or Greek, uses a term which in that language and culture is gender inclusive, as in Hebrew "sons" can refer to sons and daughters, then in the receptor language, English, the translator must decide if the closest formal equivalent, the English word "sons," is the best rendering. If the translator thinks that "sons" in English is too gender specific to capture what the donor word means in that context, he or she may judge that some such rendering as "sons and daughters" is more faithful to the Hebrew source than the word "sons" would be.

None of this is new. The additional factor that has sprung up is that most translators judge that a number of English words have become more gender specific during the past few years, and therefore faithful translation demands, in such cases, fewer formal equivalents and more semantic equivalents (that is, equivalents in meaning). There was a time, of course, when almost any competent speaker of English would have told you that the word "man" means different things in different passages. In some contexts "man" refers to a male, or to all males, of the human species. In such passages, the context discloses that the word "man" is gender specific. But in some other contexts, those English speakers would have told you, the same word "man" has generic force that includes all human beings, male and female, without distinction. In such contexts, the word "man" is gender inclusive.

For the past quarter of a century or so, however, this usage has increasingly come under attack. Critics note that the word "man" never refers exclusively to the female of the species. If such usage, alternating between the male and the generic, is not concrete evidence of male oppression, it is argued, at the very least it is insensitive. The result has been some shift in usage. And the same is true for a range of other nouns and pronouns that flip back and forth between the gender-specific male and the generic.

How much of a shift has actually taken place is one of the things that is disputed: I shall return to this point in chapter 9. For the moment, I shall assume that a real shift has occurred. The perception of such a shift has been strong enough that it has prompted several groups to work on Bible translations that accommodate this change in contemporary English usage.

In passing, I should make clear that those concerned with inclusive language come from a wide range of stances on the broader questions raised by contemporary feminism. The most radical feminists have developed liturgies that replace "Father, Son, and Holy Spirit" with "Creator, Redeemer, and Sustainer." They reason that the Bible itself was written in a culture steeped in patriarchalism, and to preserve what is essential to the Bible's message without causing needless offense, almost all the God language in the Bible and in Bible-based liturgies should be modified. Although a few liturgies in mainline denominations have adopted this stance, Bible publishers and translators have largely resisted it. Most people involved in inclusive-language Bible translation are prepared to move toward renderings that make generic uses of words like "man" and "he" explicitly inclusive—indeed, they insist that this makes Bible translations, in our culture, *more* accurate than they would otherwise be. But they are unwilling to tamper with language that refers to God. Their reasons we shall look at later. At the moment, it is enough to observe that *none* of the well-known Bible translations that have opted for inclusive language have systematically tried to emasculate references to God as Father or to Jesus as Son. With only rare exceptions, some of which I shall evaluate in chapter 8, the passages at issue do not affect how God or Jesus is presented.

Some Historical Perspective

Long before the present controversy erupted, Bible translators had to struggle with when they should choose inclusive language and when they should not. The first printed English New Testament was translated by William Tyndale and published in 1526. Judgments in the arena of gender systems had to be made. In Matthew 5:9, for instance, Tyndale rendered the text, "Blessed are the peacemakers, for they shall be called the *children* of God," even though the underlying Greek word is *huioi*, that is, "sons." "Children" remained the preferred rendering until the ASV (1901) and the NKJV (1982). In fact, the KJV renders the Hebrew word *bēn* (or its plural *bānîm*) as "son" or "sons" 2,822 times and as "child" or "children" 1,533 times, or about 35 percent.[3]

Even more striking is the fact that this sort of shift occasionally occurs when an Old Testament text is quoted in the New Testament. In 2 Samuel 7, God tells David, through Nathan the prophet, how Solomon will succeed him and build the temple that David wanted to build. Referring to Solomon, God says, "I will be a Father to him, and he will be a son to me" (7:14, author's translation). This Father/son relationship becomes a pattern for God's relationship to the Davidic king, not least the ultimate Davidic king. For instance, Psalm 2 is the first place where the Hebrew word for messiah is explicitly linked with the son of David, and here too God ties the appointment of the Davidic king, his enthronement, to the establishment of the Father/son relationship (Ps. 2:7). The apostle Paul also picks up 2 Samuel 7:14. In the context, he is arguing that believers should live separately from the world (2 Cor.

6:14–7:1). He advances several arguments and quotes several Old Testament texts, the last of which is 2 Samuel 7:14, which he renders, "I will be a Father to you, and you shall be sons and daughters to me" (2 Cor. 6:18, author's translation).

Note carefully what the apostle Paul has done. He has taken the third-person singular (*"he* will be a *son* to me") and rewritten it as a second-person plural—not only a second-person plural, but in terms that expand the masculine "son" into both genders: *"you* shall be *sons and daughters* to me.*"* Nor is it the case in this passage that Paul is simply citing the common Greek version—some form of the Septuagint (LXX)—without worrying too much about the details, for here the LXX follows the Hebrew rather closely. Nor can one easily imagine that Paul was ignorant of the Hebrew and LXX texts. Even the more biblically literate in the Corinthian congregation would have been familiar with at least the Greek text, so they would have detected the changes Paul has introduced.

I shall briefly return to this passage in chapter 8. There are complex reasons why Paul can argue this way, bound up with an important typology that needs to be explored. But the least we can say is that the apostle himself does not think that Hebrew singulars must always be rendered by Greek singulars, or that the Hebrew "son" should never be rendered by the Greek "sons and daughters." No one, I think, would quickly charge Paul with succumbing to a feminist agenda.

Not that Paul was the first to make such adjustments. The Septuagint itself also on occasion moves in the direction of gender-inclusive translation. The Bible tells us that Hosea's wife Gomer bore three children, two sons and one daughter (Hosea 1). The Hebrew of Hosea 2:4 (2:6 MT), however, literally says, "Upon her *sons* also I will have no pity, because they are *sons* of whoredom." We do not have to wait for modern translations before we find the formal equivalent dropped in favor of the semantic equivalent: not only do we find "children" in the KJV, ASV, NIV, NRSV, and most other English translations, but the same shift was accomplished in the Septuagint

(Hosea 2:6 LXX), which uses a Greek neuter word for "children" instead of the common Greek word for "sons." This is competent translation; it is certainly not the product of a feminist agenda.

Recent Developments

So what is new about the current developments in inclusive-language translations? At one level, as we have seen, nothing is new: those who translate ancient languages into English have always wrestled with these sorts of questions. Moreover, as we shall see in chapter 4, translation from almost any language to almost any other language involves some hard choices in this area. Nevertheless, there are two new developments. First, owing to continuing shifts in English usage that make more and more words gender specific, for the first time Bible translation committees have tried to work out systematic principles in this area and then apply them to the whole Bible.[4] In the past, such questions were largely dealt with in an ad hoc way. Now they are being worked out systematically. If you like the results, you will conclude that this brings about consistency; if you do not like the results, you will conclude that something artificial is being imposed on the text. Second, because these shifts in the language have come about, not so much because of unidentified linguistic developments of a haphazard sort, but at least in part because of social agendas strongly advocated by feminist thinkers of various stripes, these translational questions have become freighted with more significance than they would otherwise enjoy. This is true for both sides of the debate: if some feminists and egalitarians see these linguistic changes as something to be espoused and promoted, some complementarians see them as something to be repulsed at all costs. As a result it is becoming more and more difficult to engage in cool evaluation of the translational factors involved without soon becoming enmeshed in debates about motives, social change, and biblical fidelity.

Still, it must be said that several inclusive-language Bibles appeared without much fuss. In most cases one can offer an intelligent guess as to why their publication elicited relatively little comment. The Revised English Bible (REB), published in 1989 by both Oxford University Press and Cambridge University Press, declared in its preface, "The use of male-oriented language, in passages of traditional versions of the Bible which evidently apply to both genders, has become a sensitive issue in recent years; the revisers have preferred more inclusive gender reference where that has been possible without compromising scholarly integrity or English style." Similarly, "thou" and related forms were abandoned in direct address to God. But the REB is a revision of the New English Bible (NEB). Three factors ensured that neither the NEB nor the REB would become the Bible of the people. (1) The English is elegant, the vocabulary large, the style impressive—characteristics that attract the best-educated people in the English-speaking world, but no one else. (2) More important, the NEB adopted critical stances toward the Bible with which virtually no confessional Christian could feel comfortable, including more than one hundred textual displacements in the Old Testament that had no textual warrant whatsoever but were made purely on "higher critical" grounds. The most egregious features of the NEB have been rectified in the REB, which in fact reads very smoothly. (3) Nevertheless, both the NEB and the REB stand far enough away from traditional language in many passages that some Christians, steeped in the tradition of, say, the KJV, or even the RSV, find that distance a little off-putting. Certainly the NEB has enjoyed only a fraction of the sales of, say, the NIV,[5] and the REB is not going to reverse this trend. Thus, if conservative believers were aware of the REB's existence, they were unlikely to object very loudly, simply because it belonged to a small constituency far removed from them and therefore offering no threat.

The Contemporary English Version (CEV), published by Thomas Nelson in 1995 under the sponsorship of the American Bible Society, is described as a "user-friendly" and a "mission-driven" translation "that can be *read aloud* without stumbling, *heard* without misunderstanding, and *listened to* with enjoyment and appreciation, because the language is contemporary and the style is lucid and lyrical."[6] Like the REB, it employs gender-inclusive language fairly extensively. Its publication history is still very recent. Its popular level of writing has ensured its adoption by some popular parachurch ministries, including some conservative ones. No attention was drawn, in the Thomas Nelson edition, to its gender-inclusive translation policy, and one suspects that some of these parachurch ministries had not even noticed this feature of this version until the current crisis blew up. Something similar could be said for NIrV, the NIV that was recast for young children and other readers with limited vocabulary and reading skills.

The New Living Translation (NLT), the 1996 update of the extraordinarily popular Living Bible (LB), similarly adopted "gender-inclusive language." Its introduction provides examples of how this policy works out. For example, a traditional rendering of Proverbs 22:6 might read, "Train up a child in the way *he* should go, and when *he* is old *he* will not depart from it." The NLT offers, "Teach your children to choose the right path, and when they are older, they will remain upon it"—in this case avoiding the masculine pronoun by switching to plural. But the NLT, despite its largely conservative constituency, did not immediately come under attack. Partly this sprang from the fact that both the LB and the NLT advertise themselves as paraphrases—or, more precisely, the LB advertises itself as a paraphrase, and the NLT presents itself as a "thought-for-thought" translation. Whatever the label, most readers do not expect quite the same degree of rigor from Bibles in that tradition. Moreover, although many copies of the LB (and one suspects this will be true of the NLT) are cherished for personal reading, it is far from clear that the NLT will overtake the NIV as a standard pew Bible.

There are several other gender-inclusive Bible translations, most of which will receive little notice in this book. The most sophisticated gender-inclusive translation is the New Revised Standard Version (NRSV), published in 1989. This is a revision of the Revised Standard Version (RSV). Whatever its theological proclivities, it therefore stands in a tradition that prefers formal equivalents where possible, and proves less free than, say, the NIV, let alone the REB or the NLT. The maxim the committee followed was "As literal as possible, as free as necessary."[7] Like the REB, it eliminates all archaizing forms of English ("thou," "hadst," etc.). And it too espouses gender-inclusive principles throughout the translation where words referring to human beings are understood by the translators to be generic in meaning.[8]

Quite apart from the gender issue, many of the NRSV's renderings are distinct improvements over the RSV. Some of these reflect changes in English usage. "I will accept no bull from your house" (RSV) may have been acceptable in 1952, but today "I will not accept a bull from your house" (NRSV) is decidedly superior. Similarly, "Once I was stoned" (RSV) has understandably given way to "Once I received a stoning"—though "to receive a stoning" somehow seems to downplay the experience.

The NRSV systematically adopts a gender-inclusive expression when the donor expression is judged generic. On the whole, the committee's efforts avoid the most obvious traps. For example, in the parables of Jesus if a "man" is doing something that only a male would do in that culture, the English word "man" is retained (for example, Matt. 25:14). Masculine pronouns for Deity are thinned out, but not neutered and not feminized. Nevertheless, the policy of adopting gender-inclusive language is systematically worked out. Various devices are employed. Thus, in Mark 2:27, another word replaces "man": it now reads, "The Sabbath was made for humankind, not humankind for the Sabbath." Sometimes expressions are pluralized: instead of "Blessed is the man who walks not in the counsel of the wicked"

(RSV), we now have "Happy are those who do not follow the advice of the wicked." "Fathers" often becomes "ancestors," "brothers" regularly becomes "brothers and sisters." In Ezekiel, where *ben-ʾādām* ("son of man") occurs about ninety times, the NRSV opts for "mortal." Occasionally the translators change to another person to avoid gender-specific language: for example, Psalm 41:5 RSV, "My enemies say in malice, 'When will he [that is, the psalmist] die, and his name perish?'" becomes in the NRSV "My enemies wonder in malice when I will die, and my name perish"—since "I" is gender neutral while "he" is not. The direct speech of the enemies, of course, is thereby lost. In a few instances, such metamorphoses threatened so much havoc that the translators admit they threw up their hands in despair and left the offending masculine pronoun in place (for example, Psalm 109).

Various criticisms can be leveled, of course: we'll come to those in due course. In fairness, it should be pointed out that some critics on the more radical feminist wing think that the NRSV is not nearly radical enough. They want to eliminate, for instance, any male reference to God. We shall reflect on both the demand and the restraint in due course. A few critics charge the NRSV with inadequately pursuing its stated policy. For example, Acts 15:1 NRSV still preserves "brothers," and this has been criticized: "Then certain individuals came down from Judea and were teaching *the brothers,* 'Unless you are circumcised according to the custom of Moses, you cannot be saved.' " But here the NRSV's restraint is wholly admirable: can you imagine the national snicker if the text read that those from Judea were teaching *the brothers and sisters* that they had to be circumcised?

Once again there was little fuss. A few sign wavers protested outside the hotel at the Society of Biblical Literature when the NRSV was unveiled and reviewed in that venue. The advertising was such that anyone who was awake could scarcely have failed to take note that the NRSV employs gender-inclusive language. I suspect that this version did not draw the opposition of conservatives because it is sponsored by the Division of Christian Education of the National Council of the Churches of Christ (NCCC), so that many evangelicals, especially those in independent churches and in evangelical denominations that are mostly outside the NCCC, could dismiss the effort with a weary, "What else could you expect?"

The restraint (or indifference?) dissolved when the New International Version (NIV) headed down a similar (though slightly more restrained) path. The NIV is the best-selling English version of the Bible in the world, widely judged to be suitable for both church and private use. It is especially appreciated in evangelical circles. Since its first appearance, the Committee on Bible Translation (CBT), a group of fifteen scholars from many denominations, has continued to receive suggestions for the improvement of the NIV. They are committed to the task of continuing to keep the NIV in contemporary English and faithful to the source texts. In the 1980s they had produced an edition with minor changes. Contemplating the next set of changes, in 1992 they decided to provide an inclusive-language edition.

One of their first tasks was to adopt a set of principles.[9] Among the most important were the following: retain the gender used in the original words referring to God, angels, and demons; gender-specific features in such literary genres as parables and exemplary stories were not to be changed without good reason; the feminine gender of cities and states or nations would be retained; on the other hand, not only would generic uses for formally male terms be rendered by some gender-neutral expression, but sometimes an expression such as "workman" might become "worker" if it is established that the "work" involved could in that culture be done by a man or a woman; masculine singular pronouns such as "he" that were contextually gender inclusive could be pluralized to get around the problem; and so forth.

Market research prompted the American publisher, Zondervan, to proceed slowly. In 1996, however, the British publisher, Hodder and Stoughton, brought out the NIVI—the NIV in its gender-inclusive edition. That edition cannot legally be sold in the United States.

Included in the preface to this edition is a sentence that could be interpreted in two quite different ways: "At the same time, it was recognised that it was often appropriate to mute the patriarchalism of the culture of the biblical writers through gender-inclusive language when this could be done without compromising the message of the Spirit."

1. Taken in the strictest sense, this sentence was bound to set alarm bells ringing among complementarians: it sounds as if wherever the Bible says something that our culture views as too "patriarchal," we have every right to dismiss what it says as a vestige of an outmoded view we have outgrown. So we ignore what the text says and listen to a rather vague "message of the Spirit."

2. Alternatively, it is possible to read the sentence in a minimalist sense: "the patriarchalism of the culture" refers to no more than the prevalence of gender-inclusive expressions in, say, Hebrew, whose formal equivalents in English may be gender specific, prompting sensitive translators, rightly understanding what God by his Spirit has actually said in the Word, to seek greater accuracy by looking for gender-inclusive expressions in the receptor language.

As I read the sentence when it is pulled out of its paragraph, it seems to favor the first view; when I restore it to its paragraph, it can comfortably be understood in the second sense, since the next sentence goes on to explain: "This involved distinguishing between those passages in which an activity was normally carried out by either males or females, and other cases where the gender of the people concerned was less precisely identified. While in cases of the former the text could be left unaltered, in cases of the latter words like 'workmen' could be changed to 'worker' or 'craftsman' to 'skilled worker.'"

Or again, the statement in question could be taken as meaning something between these two alternatives. For example, it has long been recognized that the precise form of a biblical mandate may be so cloaked in a cultural peculiarity that it is not to be obeyed *in that form*. "Greet one another with a holy kiss" does not mean that the apostle is providing us with a theology of kissing: the form of greeting may be highly diverse, but the apostle's point in any case has to do with the warmth of the fellowship of believers and the way they are to receive and welcome and forbear with one another. In that case, of course, one must articulate principles that enable you to distinguish when a biblical mandate is to be obeyed in precisely the form in which it is cast, or in the cultural equivalent. This is not the place to unpack those principles: I shall say a little more along these lines in chapter 5. Among the principles, obviously, is whether the Bible displays an interest in the particular form (in this case, kissing) or focuses primary theological attention on the undergirding attitude.[10] Certainly some have tried to argue that whatever patriarchalism there is in the Bible is nothing more than an inevitable cultural residue. Others have argued that, however much we rightly insist that both sexes are of equal importance, equally human, and equally significant, role distinctions between men and women are part of a sustained theological picture that is universally binding on the human race. Does the sentence in the NIVI's preface address that debate?

The statement in the preface to the NIVI is so plastic that with a little effort it could be made to fit almost anywhere along the spectrum I've just laid out. Certainly it is not a high-water mark of clarity; inevitably, it has fueled the worst fears of complementarians. At the very least, however, all sides should recognize that the CBT members include both complementarians and egalitarians.

The Current Crisis

What ignited the flame of indignation and condemnation, inaugurating the brouhaha, was an article by Susan Olasky in *World*. This conservative magazine advertises itself as a weekly news magazine like *Time* or *Newsweek,* but something you can trust. The front cover for March 29, 1997, features a Bible with a red sign for the female along the spine, and the shadow of a stealth aircraft draped across the leather binding. The words read: "The Stealth Bible: The Popular *New International Version* Bible Is Quietly Going 'Gender-Neutral.'" The article itself is titled "The Feminist Seduction of the Evangelical Church: Femme Fatale."[11]

The opening paragraph asserts that by the year 2000 or 2001—"if the 15-member Committee for Biblical Translation (CBT) . . . has its way"—we will no longer be able to purchase a copy of the NIV we now know: only the NIVI will be available. The next paragraph concedes that this may not happen: Zondervan may choose to put out two separate editions. Author Olasky keeps referring to the "unisex language" in the NIVI. There is no discussion of translation theory or of the extent to which gender-inclusive language has cropped up during the previous two thousand and more years. The drive toward the NIVI is attributed to the perceived shift in language usage, generated by feminists, and to the concern of the British publishers that the NRSV was eating into the NIV markets. Precisely three passages in the NRSV are discussed to illustrate how the use of gender-inclusive language can affect the meaning of a passage:

> The NRSV includes passages that are tortured ("Let us make humankind in our own image. . . . So God created humankind," Genesis 1:26). It includes passages that are historically misleading ("The warriors who went out to battle," Numbers 31:28; those warriors were men, according to the Hebrew). It includes passages that are doctrinally confusing ("What are human beings that you are mindful of them or mortals that you care for them," Hebrews 2:5; in the book of Hebrews, this passage refers to Christ).[12]

The next third of the article says nothing about translations, except to say that the publication of the NIVI "fits with the trend toward egalitarianism," and then demonstrates this by talking about Willow Creek Community Church in South Barrington, Illinois.[13] Willow Creek has had women elders since 1978, but it has allowed its members and staff to disagree with the policy. In January 1996 one of the teaching elders, John Ortberg, taught a class and distributed a paper demanding that staff come into line with the egalitarian position of the church or study until they did—and they had a year to do so. (The year is now up, and discipline is being imposed.) Developments at Willow Creek are then charted. Somewhat similar debates at Park Street Church in Boston, Massachusetts, are briefly canvassed.

Most of the rest of Olasky's article interacts with the opinions of Dr. Dan Doriani, dean of faculty at Covenant Theological Seminary in St. Louis, and of Dr. R. Albert Mohler, president of Southern Baptist Theological Seminary. There is a little interaction with Dr. Gilbert Bilezikian, a leader on the egalitarian side of the debate and perhaps the major theological voice behind Willow Creek, and a brief comment from Dr. Wayne Grudem of the Council on Biblical Manhood and Womanhood (CBMW).

That was it.

And this time there were major statements, debates, and in a few cases uncontrolled rage.

Two weeks later, on April 19, 1997, *World* published two more articles. The one by Susan Olasky begins with several paragraphs describing the wealth of Zondervan Corporation, asserting that this wealth derives from publishing the NIV and, to a lesser extent, the NRSV. Zondervan, *World* reports, had not noted any "factual inaccuracies" in the original *World* article but had criticized *World*'s tone and methodology. Zondervan had published a statement asserting "we intend in no way to advance a particular social agenda or stray from the original biblical texts." Zondervan's director of corporate affairs, Jonathan Petersen, is reported as charging that the terms "inclusive," "unisex," and "gender-neutral" are unfair: "We would characterize it as the 'gender-accurate version.'"

The article makes it reasonably clear that at the time, although the American edition of the NIVI was not yet in the publication pipeline, and although no final decision regarding its publication had been taken, the project was apparently going ahead. Olasky suggests that Zondervan's commitments are disclosed in their own editing guidelines (which are gender inclusive), the fact that Zondervan was already publishing the NIrV and NRSV, and Zondervan's contractual arrangements with the Committee on Bible Translation. Featured prominently were comments by Dr. J. I. Packer: "Adjustments made by what I call the feminist edition are not made in the interests of legitimate translation procedure. These changes have been made to pander to a cultural prejudice that I hope will be short-lived."

The second article published in that issue of *World* was written by Dr. Wayne Grudem, professor of biblical and systematic theology at Trinity Evangelical Divinity School and president of the Council on Biblical Manhood and Womanhood. It briefly compares the NIV and the NIVI on a number of biblical passages, and comments on the difference. In each case the format is the same. One example will suffice, since some of the other passages will be discussed later in this book.

Text: John 14:23

Current NIV: If anyone loves me, he will obey my teaching. My Father will love him, and we will come to him and make our home with him.

Inclusive Language NIV: Those who love me will obey my teaching. My Father will love them, and we will come to them and make our home with them.

Change in Meaning: Dwelling of Father and Son with individual person is lost; new NIV speaks of Father and Son dwelling among a group of people. Six singular

Greek words which John wrote as part of Scripture are mistranslated in this one text.[14]

Other voices quickly weighed in. For example, Dr. Paige Patterson, president of Southeastern Baptist Theological Seminary, wrote an article for Dr. Jerry Falwell's *National Liberty Journal*. This article summarized Olasky's article, but in somewhat more passionate prose.[15] On April 28, Dr. Kenneth L. Barker, secretary of the Committee on Bible Translation and himself a committed complementarian, wrote me a letter asking if I would respond to some of these articles with an article of my own. He knew, of course, that I too am a complementarian, was at that time on the Board of Reference of CBMW, and had been involved in various ways with the theory and practice of translation. Perceiving that what I would say would probably not satisfy anyone, disliking a controversy which in my view was moving in unprofitable directions, and above all being swamped with other responsibilities, I delayed responding while I thought it over.

On May 14, IBS and Zondervan released a joint statement announcing that they are "unequivocally committed to continue to publish the current NIV text, without any changes or revisions." At the same time, they would "continue to move forward with plans for the possible publication of an updated edition of the present NIV," not earlier than 2001. The announcement explains these potentially conflicting statements. If a new edition is produced (and sooner or later it will be), the present NIV will nevertheless remain in print. In other words, a potential new edition will not replace the current NIV in Zondervan's publishing schedule.

Pressure continued to mount. Only weeks before their annual convention, Southern Baptist leaders not only condemned the "unisex" NIVI but predicted serious action at the forthcoming annual meeting. IBS and Zondervan leaders met with some Southern Baptist leaders on May 19 in Nashville. David C. Cook Church Ministries, which publishes a great deal of Sunday School material, was reportedly looking again at their commitment to the NIrV. James Dobson of Focus on the Family intervened. On May 3 he had written a column in *World* warning against "injecting feminist bias and language into the inspired text." Then Focus discovered that its own *Odyssey Bible* for children used gender-inclusive language. Focus promptly withdrew that edition and offered a full refund of the purchase price. In due course Dobson invited the NIV/NIVI publishers to meet with him and some theologians, not least those most critical of the NIVI.

Three days before that meeting, I was phoned by one of the participants and asked to go along. Unable to set aside other responsibilities, I declined. From Focus, Dr. James Dobson attended, as did Mr. Charlie Jarvis, executive vice president. Those who attended on the one side were Dr. Kenneth Barker, secretary of the CBT; Dr. Ronald Youngblood, one of the CBT members;[16] Dr. Lars Dunberg, president of IBS; and Mr. Bruce Ryskamp, president and CEO of Zondervan. On the other side were Mr. Joel Belz, publisher of *World;* Dr. Wayne Grudem, president of CBMW; Mr. Tim Bayly, executive director of CBMW; Dr. R. C. Sproul of Ligonier Ministries, a member of CBMW's Board of Reference; Dr. Vern Poythress of Westminster Theological Seminary; and Dr. John Piper, senior pastor of Bethlehem Baptist Church and coeditor, with Dr. Wayne Grudem, of *Recovering Biblical Manhood and Womanhood: A Response to Evangelical Feminism.*[17]

The day before the Focus meeting itself, planned for Tuesday, May 27, these latter scholars met in a Colorado Springs Marriott. They compiled a ten-page list of NIVI mistranslations (as they took them to be), constructed a set of alternative guidelines for translators dealing with gender-oriented problems, and made a list of the commitments they wanted the publishers to make. They finished their task at 2:00 A.M. and met with the entire group at 9:00 A.M. the next day.

Battered by the adverse publicity, not least among Southern Baptists, two hours before the meeting in Colorado Springs on May 27, IBS released a four-point policy statement to the effect that

- IBS has abandoned all plans for gender-related changes in future editions of the New International Version (NIV).
- The present (1984) NIV text will continue to be published. There are no plans for a further revised edition.
- IBS will begin immediately to revise the New International Readers Version (NIrV) in a way that reflects the treatment of gender in the NIV. IBS is directing the licensees who publish the current NIrV to publish only the revised NIrV edition as soon as it is ready.
- IBS will enter into negotiations with the publisher of the NIV in the U.K. on the matter of ceasing publication of its "inclusive language" edition of the NIV.

Thus some of the primary concerns of the critics were already met. Afraid of losing its market, while doubtless wanting to be loyal to its constituency, neither Zondervan nor IBS had much room to maneuver. IBS and Zondervan admitted to some mistakes in the NIVI. Dr. Kenneth Barker had prepared a revised set of guidelines which in partial measure paralleled what the critics were proposing. Before they left the meeting, everyone agreed in principle on a joint statement. Dr. Ronald Youngblood had left the meeting early. When the gender-language document was shown to him, he declared he could not sign it as it was, but agreed to do so a few days later, after a substantial number of qualifiers had been inserted: note the frequency of expressions such as "often," "only rare exceptions," "ordinarily," "unusual exceptions." In addition, some clauses were rewritten to allow a trifle more flexibility. The resulting document, both in that form and in a form slightly revised once again, has been so widely published (and I have printed it again in chapter 2) that I need not summarize its principal points here.

The critics have ranged from being very pleased to frankly jubilant. In the latter category was the cover story for the June 14/21 issue of *World,* titled "Bailing Out of the Stealth Bible."[18] The tone in the June issue of *CBMW News* was more restrained. In essence, it saw all the developments as the sure hand of God and emphasized the depth of the agreement, in a godly spirit, on all fronts. That was not quite how the other side saw things. Several individuals both in the CBT and in the administration of the publishers have described a less harmonious picture but wanted to keep a low profile because of the politics of the situation. Zondervan sent a ten-page ethics complaint to a committee of the Evangelical Press Association criticizing the series of articles in *World,* a complaint that eventually petered out. For myself, I was not there. I have listened to friends from both sides of the debate describe what happened, and it is difficult to align the two sets of pictures.

In some ways that was not the end of the struggle but the beginning. Late spring and early summer annual meetings of various denominational groups, including the Southern Baptist Convention and the Presbyterian Church in America, passed resolutions vowing to oppose gender-inclusive Bible translations. Various news magazines and journals kept the issue alive. Some scholars felt constrained to resign from the Board of Reference of CBMW, not because they disagreed with the complementarianism CBMW has defended, but because they disagreed (1) with its tightly linking the issue of complementarianism to that of gender-inclusive translations and (2) with at least some of the principles the critics had advanced in Colorado Springs and which CBMW subsequently endorsed.[19] In mid-July *Christianity Today* published a photograph of Dean Merrill, IBS vice president, holding one of several NIV Bibles that had been destroyed by a drill. Bible rage had struck.

A quiet but rising chorus of publishers and Bible translators began to reflect on the Colorado Springs principles and ask technical questions. Doubtless some of these questions were mooted by egalitarians, but it would be grossly unfair to suggest they were the only ones doing so. Executives from Wycliffe Bible Translators, International Bible Society, United Bible Societies, the Bible League, Thomas Nelson, Tyndale House Publishers, and Zondervan Publishing House began to lay plans for a broad-based conference of scholars and Bible translators to discuss these issues and perhaps generate a set of guidelines.[20] At the end of July, Mark D. Taylor of Tyndale House Publishers circulated a memo to everyone who had worked on the NLT. He defended the "moderate" use of gender-inclusive language and expressed his dissatisfaction with some of the Focus principles. Nevertheless, Tyndale House Publishers has obviously learned something from the controversy: Mr. Taylor also indicated some changes that would be introduced into future printings of the NLT. Meanwhile Christians for Biblical Equality, an egalitarian group, collected signatures for its protest to IBS.

The October 27 issue of *Christianity Today* carried an article by Dr. Wayne Grudem and another by Dr. Grant Osborne, along with their respective responses to each other. Dr. Grudem argues that inclusive-language translations distort Scripture; Dr. Osborne says that this is not necessarily the case, arguing that a good grasp of translation theory establishes his position. The same issue includes a two-page ad summarizing the Focus meeting and translation principles, and including the names of all those who had been present, plus an impressive list of names of others who had subsequently endorsed the principles. I gather, however, that Bruce E. Ryskamp (president and CEO of Zondervan) and Lars Dunberg (president of IBS) did not want their names to be used, not least because both of them publish other inclusive-language versions of the Bible. They therefore explicitly asked that their names be removed from similar ads in later publications.

Most of the men[21] who signed this document[22] are known to me personally; not a few are friends. I have no desire to alienate any of them. And yet as I look at the list, I cannot help but conclude that what drew many of them to sign this document is their concern to maintain complementarianism, and this out of strong biblical convictions, and their belief that the question of gender-inclusive translations is a necessary component of this conviction. Quite a number of them, I think, would make no pretense of having much grasp of Hebrew, Aramaic, Greek, translation theory, and linguistics. Would it not be fair to suggest that at least some signed the document because of their concern over the larger issue and their trust in the framers of the document? What then shall we do who share their larger concern but are persuaded neither that the published guidelines of the CBT are sufficiently careful nor that the principles agreed on at Colorado Springs are always soundly based? The issues are complex, and we need cool heads and more time to get this one right. Slogans and demonizing those who disagree with us will not help.

Concluding Reflections

But enough. What we must see is that, while on all sides of this debate there are some passionate people—some of them enraged—there are also some people who are extraordinarily self-disciplined and gracious, and many who are between the extremes. The diversity and intensity of the reactions are in one sense a good thing: important issues should not be laughed off as of no moment. Nevertheless, history offers many examples of movements which, seeking to head off a genuine evil in the culture, unwittingly swing the pendulum to unseen evils on the other side. In large part this little book is nothing more than an attempt to lower the temperature, slow the pace of debate, and bring up some things that, in my view, are sometimes overlooked.

To close this lengthy report on this confrontation, I wish to summarize a small part of a discussion between Dr. Kenneth

Barker and Dr. Wayne Grudem on *Open Line,* a radio program produced by Moody, aired May 13, 1997. Dr. Grudem raises John 14:23 (cited in the excerpt above), saying that the change from the repeated singular references to the plural "we will come to *them* and make our home with *them*" has the effect of losing the personal application. The text may now mean no more than that the Father and the Son will live among all the believers, rather than with the individual believer. Dr. Barker responds that we are accustomed to many plurals from which we automatically make a personal application. For example, in Matthew 5:6, Jesus says, "Blessed are *those* who hunger and thirst for righteousness, for *they* will be filled." Each individual believer applies such texts to himself or herself individually. So why treat the plurals in the NIVI of John 14:23 as a serious problem in which individual application will be lost? Dr. Grudem replies that he has no problem with plurals that can be read individually. His point, he says, is that in John 14:23 the inspired author does *not* use a plural, and therefore we should not do so either. Dr. Barker says that the singular in John 14:23 is clearly generic, and therefore faithful, accurate translation *demands* that we use the plural form, or some other way of avoiding a rendering that unnecessarily repulses some readers with its maleness, because some readers will find such words exclusive. Dr. Grudem replies that our first allegiance is to Scripture, and the issue at stake is one of accuracy. If John chooses to use the singular, he had reasons for doing so, and we should not quickly sacrifice what the text actually says.

Both parties are claiming to be faithful and accurate; both sides are saying, in effect, that the other is fundamentally mistaken. Where do we go from here?

2

CONFLICTING PRINCIPLES

THE CBT AND CSG
ON INCLUSIVE LANGUAGE

For the sake of easy reference, it will prove useful to set out the policy of the Committee on Bible Translation (CBT) that stands behind the NIVI, along with the guidelines agreed on in Colorado Springs. At this juncture I am attempting no systematic evaluation. That will come later in the book. Nevertheless, a couple of explanatory comments may prove helpful.

First, the CBT policy, adopted in August 1992, is a published statement open to inspection. I am grateful to Professor John Stek, the chair of the CBT, for sending me a copy. But it is common knowledge that the CBT is currently preparing a revised set of guidelines. As these are still being worked on, they are viewed as confidential, and neither Professor Stek nor anyone else with whom I talked felt comfortable about showing them to me. One understands their reluctance: at this point the committee is doubtless a trifle gun-shy. An optimistic reading of these circumstances is that in the mercy of God the controversy may help sharpen thinking in this area: the principles adopted at Colorado Springs may help to shape the thinking of the CBT, even if the latter cannot go all the way with the former. We must avoid entrenched thinking and conspiracy theories: let us learn from one another, not least those with whom we disagree.

Second, the policy agreed on in Colorado Springs needs a name. We might call it the Focus on the Family policy, but Focus was the sponsoring organization, not the brains behind the formulation of the policy. In an earlier draft, I called it the CBMW policy. Although scholars other than those affiliated with CBMW were involved in the formulation of that policy, the CBMW tag seemed appropriate for two reasons. (1) CBMW was the organization most strongly represented in the ad hoc group of scholars that met in the Colorado Springs Marriott. (2) More important, CBMW has not only promoted the principles most strongly but has apparently organized their upgrade. Strictly speaking, the slightly modified principles now being circulated are not exactly the ones agreed on in Colorado Springs (though we are told that the original signers have agreed to the changes).[1] But others signed the document, and in consultation with two or three of the framers, I learned of their strong preference for "Colorado Springs Guidelines" (CSG) or the Colorado Springs (CS) principles—though of course all sides recognize that the geography was accidental. So CSG or CS principles it is.

It is surely encouraging, not least for those who oppose the CSG, that CBMW leaders and others related to them are willing to modify their views. Perhaps further modifications are possible. Once again, the issues are too complicated to be well treated by entrenched thinking and simplistic "good guys versus bad guys" or "them versus us" analyses. Doubtless points of disagreement will remain, but it is important to push toward as much agreement as we can manage.

So here, then, are the two sets of guidelines, the respective gender-language policies of the CBT and CS.

CBT Policy on Gender-Inclusive Language[2]

I. Basic Principles

M[oved]S[econded and]C[arried] that these be adopted as amended:

A. Biblical translations must be faithful to the original language texts out of fidelity to the Word of God.

B. Biblical translation is for the purpose of making the Word of God available to all who know the receptor language—so that they all can "take and read"—women and men alike.

C. Authors of Biblical books, even while writing Scripture inspired by the Holy Spirit, unconsciously reflected in many ways, the particular cultures in which they wrote. Hence in the manner in which they articulate the Word of God, they sometimes offend modern sensibilities. At such times, translators can and may use non-offending renderings so as not to hinder the message of the Spirit.[3]

D. The patriarchalism (like other social patterns) of the ancient cultures in which the Biblical books were composed is pervasively reflected in forms of expression that appear, in the modern context, to deny the common human dignity of all hearers and readers. For these forms, alternative modes of expression can and may be used, though care must be taken not to distort the intent of the original text.

E. Gender-inclusive language must be made in light of exegetical and linguistic attention to individual texts in their contexts; e.g., the legal and wisdom literature. In narratives, parables, exemplary stories, metaphors and the like, the gender-spe-

cific elements are usually not to be replaced or
added to in order to achieve gender balance.

F. While sexuality cannot be ascribed to God, God's
own self-descriptions and the Biblical references
to God, Satan, and angels are masculine in gender, and such references are not to be altered.

G. Nor can sexuality be ascribed to the Spirit of God,
for whom the grammatical genders of the Hebrew
and Greek terms and forms are feminine and
neuter respectively. For the sake of consistency in
references to God, masculine pronouns will be
used in referring to the Spirit.

II. General Guidelines
M[oved]S[econded and]C[arried] that these be adopted
as amended:

(1) Keep the NIV text to the greatest possible extent.

(2) Avoid any change that will produce ambiguity or
lack of clarity.

(3) Avoid any formulation that distorts the Biblical
representation of theological truths or the created
world.

(4) Where context clearly shows that reference is to
male(s), retain masculine references. Similarly,
where context clearly shows that reference is to
female(s), retain female references.

(5) Where the original cultural context shows a distinctively male activity (bowman, workman, oars-
man), characteristic, or relationship, male references may be retained, but if suitable alternatives
are available (such as archer, worker, rower), these
are usually to be preferred.

(6) Avoid repetitive masculine gender references
where alternative expressions are available and
appropriate.

(7) In legal texts careful distinction should be made
between laws that are male specific and those that

are not. In those that are not, inclusive language should be used.

(8) To avoid gender-specific language in general statements, a third-person sentence may be changed to second person where this adequately conveys the meaning, and a singular sentence may be recast in a plural form provided this does not obscure a significant individual reference. On the other hand, inclusive singular subjects (such as "everyone" and "whoever") may not be followed by plural pronouns (such as "they" and "their"). Any proposal that is an exception to this latter rule must be placed in the margin along with the reason.

(9) Do not employ artificial solutions in the pronominal structure, such as *ho, hish,* or the Scandinavian *hǎn.* "He or she," e.g., is cumbersome and should usually be avoided.

(10) In the use of inclusive language, avoid repetition that mars good style, such as frequent use of "someone," "person," "human(s)," "human being(s)," "humankind."

(11) In general, avoid gender-specific nouns and adjectives where acceptable alternatives are available. (Such terms as "prophetess" and the adjective "fellow-" need to be weighed carefully.)

(12) Expressions employed in common parlance in society today, even though they may seem to denote male dominance (such as "men and women," "boys and girls"), are not to be avoided.

(13) The convention in ancient wisdom literature of addressing young men on the threshold of adult responsibilities and the fact that certain passages in Proverbs deal with distinctly male circumstances are not to be obscured. At the same time, any individual proverbs that may have pertained to women also can be rendered inclusively.

(14) Preserve the similarity of parallel passages and quotations, and safeguard canonical unity.

(15) Feminine gender references to cities and states/nations are to be retained.

(16) Consistency within books, corpora, genres, and conventional idioms is to be maintained.

(17) When change to inclusive language requires the recasting of whole phrases or clauses, care is to be taken to retain as much continuity with the present text of the NIV as good style will allow.

(18) The language of the sectional headings must also be examined and revised where appropriate.

(19) Where gender-inclusive language is contextually inappropriate, an explanatory footnote may be called for.

(20) Where male-specific references or masculine-gender grammatical forms in the original texts are probably due to context, custom, culture, or the like, leave unchanged unless:

  (a) the passage is universally applicable (Luke 16:13; 17:31–33);

  (b) the extended passage loses specificity (Luke 14:31–35);

  (c) modern circumstances are universal (Matt. 10:24—perhaps with a footnote).

CS Policy on Gender-Inclusive Language[4]

A. Gender-related renderings of Biblical language which we affirm:

  1. The generic use of "he, him, his, himself" should be employed to translate generic 3rd person masculine singular pronouns in Hebrew, Aramaic and Greek. However, substantival participles such as *ho pisteuōn* can often be rendered in inclusive ways, such as "the one who believes" rather than "he who believes."

2. Person and number should be retained in translation so that singulars are not changed to plurals and third person statements are not changed to second or first person statements, with only rare exceptions required in unusual cases.

3. "Man" should ordinarily be used to designate the human race, for example in Genesis 1:26–27; 5:2; Ezekiel 29:11; and John 2:25.[5]

4. Hebrew *ʾîsh* should ordinarily be translated "man" and "men," and Greek *anēr* should almost always be so translated.

5. In many cases, *anthrōpoi* refers to people in general, and can be translated "people" rather than "men." The singular *anthrōpos* should ordinarily be translated "man" when it refers to a male human being.

6. Indefinite pronouns such as *tis* can be translated "anyone" rather than "any man."

7. In many cases, pronouns such as *oudeis* can be translated "no one" rather than "no man."

8. When *pas* is used as a substantive it can be translated with terms such as "all people" or "everyone."

9. The phrase "son of man" should ordinarily be preserved to retain intracanonical connections.

10. Masculine references to God should be retained.

B. Gender-related renderings which we will generally avoid, though there may be unusual exceptions in certain contexts:

1. "Brother" *(adelphos)* should not be changed to "brothers or sisters"; however, the plural *adelphoi* can be translated "brothers and sisters" where the context makes clear that the author is referring to both men and women.[6]

2. "Son" *(huios, bēn)* should not be changed to "child," or "sons" *(huioi)* to "children" or "sons

and daughters." (However, Hebrew *bānîm* often
means "children.")
  3. "Father" *(patēr, ʾāb)* should not be changed to
     "parent," or "fathers" to "parents" or "ancestors."
C. We understand these guidelines to be representative
   and not exhaustive, and that some details may need
   further refinement.[7]

3

TRANSLATION AND TREASON

AN INEVITABLE AND IMPOSSIBLE TASK

Traddutore, traditore: "Translators, traitors." This Italian pun insists, in effect, that all translation is treason. The pun "works" because the words for "translation" and "treason" in Italian are very similar. It doesn't work in English—which is precisely the point.

In this chapter I am stepping away from the challenges of inclusive-language translations so as to reflect a little on the nature of translation itself.

Some people innocently think that the meaning of a sentence or of a paragraph or some longer text is discovered by adding together the separate meanings of all the individual words. So translation works the same way: you translate all the words, and then add them all up again. This assumes, of course, that each word in the receptor language is more or less identical in meaning with the corresponding word in the donor language.

But discovering the meaning of a text is not anything like that, and translating a text is not anything like that. To make the point clear, this chapter offers a few examples, nothing more. Experienced translators could easily expand it into a library of books.

Differences from Language to Language

There are many, many things that separate any two languages. How great that separation is varies enormously. Here is a very partial list.

1. Two languages will vary in the most obvious way—in the meanings of the words belonging to each. Even words that are close in meaning to one another will differ at some point; in many cases, a word in one language that is properly rendered by a certain word in another language may have to be rendered by quite a different word once the context changes. The Greek verb *phileō* is often properly translated "to love," but sometimes it must be rendered "to kiss," as when Judas kissed Jesus.

2. Two languages will vary in the size of their respective vocabularies. The total lexical count of English words is about three times that of French words. In reality, of course, most English speakers and French speakers use only a small fraction of the total number of words theoretically available to them in their respective languages. Nevertheless the difference in the number of words found in any two languages provides another reason why it is impossible to map the words of one language onto the words of another. Similar things can be said for bodies of literature. The Hebrew Old Testament has just over 4,000 separate words; the Greek New Testament, which is only about one third as long, has about 5,500 words.

3. Languages have very different ways of constructing their words when they are actually being used in a context. Some

languages are "inflected": that is, they change something at the end ("suffixes"), or at the beginning ("prefixes"), or in the middle ("infixes"), or some combination of the three, depending on how those words are used. English is not a highly inflected language, but it still has occasional inflections from an earlier time. Verbs in English, in the present tense, keep the same form except for the third-person singular: for example, I run, you (singular) run, he/she/it run*s*, we run, you (plural) run, they run. Both Greek and Hebrew are highly inflected, and such changes are not restricted to verbs. In Greek, nouns have one of five formal "cases," and the right case must be chosen to align with the function of that noun in its sentence. These five cases are handled differently in the three common patterns of ending, that is, the three declensions of nouns. Verbs are "conjugated" and nouns and pronouns are "declined": thus the different "declensions" to which a noun may belong determine how its endings will change. All of this might be thought narrowly technical, of course, but it has an enormous impact on syntax, that is, on how words are linked together to generate phrases, clauses, and sentences. For example, in the simple English sentence "John loves Susan," the word order establishes who is loving (John, the subject of the verb), and who is being loved (Susan, the direct object of the verb). In Greek, of course, so far as word order is concerned, one could write "Susan loves John" and John might still be the subject, provided the word "John" is carrying the nominative case inflection, and Susan is carrying the accusative case inflection.

4. There are scores and scores of syntactical differences between Greek and English and between Hebrew and English. Hebrew employs something called an infinitive construct; there is nothing quite like it in contemporary English. First-year Greek students are taught that the prepositional Greek phrase *en tō Iōannēn exelthein* should be rendered by some such English expression as "when John went out." More precisely, the Greek preposition *en* plus the articular infinitive compounded

with an accusative is being rendered in English as a temporal subordinate clause. To translate the Greek more literally, it would come out something like "in the to go out [with respect to] John"—but of course, that is not English, so we go with the closest English equivalent we have. But in fact, Greek itself has temporal subordinate clauses: the basic thought could have been written in Greek in a way that was much closer to English syntax. That in turn raises the question of what difference in meaning there is between the two constructions in Greek. At the level of translation into English, there may be none; within Greek, of course there are differences.

5. The first languages into which the New Testament was translated differed in some major structural ways from the donor language. Latin has no article (that is, no "a" or "the"), while Greek has one. That means the significance of the article in Greek is sometimes lost when one moves to Latin; or, if its significance is not lost, it is certainly not conveyed the same way! The significance of the Greek article for English has similar problems, not because we have no article, but because we have two, and the way we use them is quite different from the way the Greek article is used. Coptic has no passive voice, like neo-Melanesian languages today. That usually means these languages have to specify a subject even when none is specified in Greek. Syriac has no subjunctive or optative mood. In other words, the kinds of problems we are talking about are not merely contemporary; they have always been there, whenever anyone has tried to translate a text from one language into another language.

6. The Hebrew verbal system is formally very simple, but it is so complicated at the level of semantics (that is, of meaning) that tomes are written on the subject, espousing theories that differ one from another. What is quite clear is that the Hebrew verbal system does not lay out time relations. Something similar can be said for part or all of the Greek system.[1] But a great deal of the English distinction of times—past, present, future, and more complicated times such as

future perfect—rides on the English verbal system. Not so in Hebrew. That does not mean that Hebrew is incapable of distinguishing times. Rather, it must do so by a variety of other means.

7. How does one translate weights and measures, dates based on quite a different calendar, money units, and times of the day, when all of these measurements are grounded in scales radically different from anything we use in English?

8. In the nature of the case, some differences between languages mean that the translator must choose between two goals: he or she cannot achieve both of them. For example, excellent Greek style puts a lot of verbs into the passive voice; excellent English style demands that we put as few as possible into the passive voice. So if we translate every Greek passive voice by a passive voice in English, we preserve the passives while sending out a signal that this is inferior English—in exactly those passages that are stylistically the best and most sophisticated Greek. We thereby lose something. Alternatively, if we switch some of the Greek passives to the active voice in English, we preserve a feel for the elegance of the Greek style by having a more elegant English. But we lose the passives.

Something similar must be said regarding Greek particles. As a rule, the more particles, the more elegant the Greek. Exactly the opposite is true in English. A choice must be made.

Quite a number of poetic passages in the Hebrew canon are acrostic poems. It is almost impossible to get that across in English. Various attempts have been made, almost always with serious loss in some other arena. There are scores of translation challenges where the translator *must* choose between two desirable things. Something will be lost. Translation is treason.

This is only a partial list of the challenges a translator faces. Perhaps a concrete example will help, one that several scholars have employed recently. It concerns the Greek word *sarx*, often rendered "flesh." Consider the following passages:

Matthew 16:17: "*sarx* and blood have not revealed this to you"
KJV/NKJV: *flesh* and blood
NASB: *flesh* and blood
NIV: this was not revealed to you by *man* [covering both "flesh and blood"]
NIVI: this was not revealed to you by *flesh* and blood
NLT: You did not learn this from any *human being*
NRSV: *flesh* and blood
REB: You did not learn that from any *human being*

Mark 14:38: "the spirit is willing, but the *sarx* is weak"
KJV/NKJV: *flesh*
NASB: *flesh*
NIV/NIVI: *body*
NLT: *body*
NRSV: *flesh*
REB: *flesh*

John 17:2: "just as you have given to him authority over all *sarx*"
KJV/NKJV: *flesh*
NASB: *mankind*
NIV/NIVI: *people*
NLT: *everyone*
NRSV: *people*
REB: *mankind*

Romans 8:6: "for the way of thinking of the *sarx* is death"
KJV/NKJV: for to be *carnally* minded is death
NASB: for the mind set on the *flesh* is death
NIV: the mind of *sinful man* is death
NIVI: the mind controlled by the *sinful nature* is death

NLT: if your *sinful nature* controls your mind, there is death

NRSV: to set the mind on the *flesh* is death

REB: those who live on the level of the *old nature* have their outlook formed from it, and that spells death [verses 5 and 6 are combined]

Romans 11:14: "if somehow I might make jealous my *sarx* and save some of them"

KJV: *them which are* my *flesh*

NKJV: *those who are* my *flesh*

NASB: *fellow countrymen*

NIV/NIVI: *own people*

NLT: *the Jews*

NRSV: *own people*

REB: *own race*

1 Corinthians 3:3: "for you are still *sarkikoi* [that is, characterized by *sarx*]"

KJV: for ye are yet *carnal*

NKJV: for you are still *carnal*

NASB: you are still *fleshly*

NIV/NIVI: you are still *worldly*

NLT: you are still controlled by your own *sinful desires*

NRSV: you are still of the *flesh*

REB: you are still on the *merely natural plane*

1 Corinthians 9:11: "is it much if we reap your *sarkika* [that is, things characterized by the *sarx*]"

KJV: reap your *carnal things*

NKJV: reap your *material things*

NASB: reap *material things* from you

NIV/NIVI: reap a *material harvest* from you

NLT: is it too much to ask, in return, for *mere food and clothing*

NRSV: reap your *material benefits*

REB: is it too much to expect from you a *material harvest*

Galatians 4:13: "because of weakness of the *sarx* I first preached the gospel to you"
KJV: through infirmity of the *flesh*
NKJV: because of *physical* infirmity
NASB: because of a *bodily* illness
NIV/NIVI: because of an *illness* [thus embracing the entire expression "weakness of the flesh"]
NLT: I was *sick*
NRSV: because of a *physical* infirmity
REB: *bodily* illness

Galatians 5:16: "walk by the Spirit and you will not fulfill the desire of the *sarx*"
KJV/NKJV: not fulfill the lust of the *flesh*
NASB: not carry out the desire of the *flesh*
NIV/NIVI: not gratify the desires of the *sinful nature*
NLT: won't be doing what your *sinful nature* craves
NRSV: do not gratify the desires of the *flesh*
REB: will not gratify the desires of your *unspiritual nature*

In Matthew 16:17, *sarx* cannot properly be evaluated by itself, because "flesh and blood" is a unit pair. The idea of "human being" is exactly what the expression means. The NIV opts for "man," but the NIVI, trying to avoid a generic use of "man," instead of opting for "human being," goes back to "flesh and blood."

The breakdown between "flesh" and "body" at Mark 14:38 may be a way of avoiding any overtones of "flesh" that are tied to sexual sin (an increasing use of the word today, as in "sins of the flesh" in modern parlance). Perhaps "body" was attractive over against "spirit." John 17:2 uses *sarx* to refer to all people. But if we do not use "flesh" to render it (for that is a fairly outmoded use of "flesh" today), any of the other options appears acceptable. In Romans 8:6

and 1 Corinthians 3:3, "carnal" or "carnally" has to go, because contemporary use has narrowed down the offense to the sexual arena. "Worldly" (NIV) is not bad, but inevitably it loses any explicit connection with the word group. Paul was certainly not trying to reap "carnal things" in the contemporary sense of "carnal" (1 Cor. 9:11). The NIV/NIVI's "material harvest" in one sense goes over the top: there is no explicit mention of harvest. Nevertheless, the word is neuter plural, and it is always a bit difficult to know how to substantivize such expressions. "Harvest" may have been judged adequate as the complement of "reap."

Or again, the word *lampros* occurs only nine times in the Greek New Testament. The KJV manages to use six different words to translate this one word (namely, "gorgeous," "bright," "goodly," "gay," "white," and "clear"), even using two different words in one passage: "For if there come unto your assembly a man with a gold ring, in *goodly* apparel, and there come in also a poor man in vile raiment; And ye have respect to him that weareth the *gay* clothing, and say unto him, Sit thou here in a good place; and say to the poor, Stand thou there, or sit here under my footstool" (James 2:2–3 KJV). Why once "goodly" and once "gay"? The words do not convey the same overtones. In any case, one could not possibly use "gay" in this context today.[2] Incidentally, the same verses employ "apparel," "raiment," and "clothing," and these three English words all have the same Greek word behind them (namely, *esthēs*).

Translators John Beekman and John Callow provide an interesting and amusing example of the way a single word in one language must be translated by many different words in another language.[3] In what follows, the first column represents a literal rendering of a number of expressions in Vagla (a tribal language in Ghana), all employing the verb "to eat" (*diy* in Vagla). The second column represents the English semantic equivalent.

Vagla Expression	English Equivalent
he ate his self	he enjoyed himself
he ate his case	he judged his case
he ate shame	he was ashamed
he ate chieftainship	he became the chief
he ate two goals	he scored two goals
he ate him a friend	he chose him as a friend
he ate him an argument	he argued with him
it is eating	it is sharp
you should eat	it's your turn

My point is that inevitably there are differences from language to language. Translation is never a merely mechanical function. It involves highly complex choices.

All of this reminds me of a funny essay Mark Twain wrote in 1875: "The 'Jumping Frog': In English, Then in French, Then Clawed Back into a Civilized Language Once More by Patient, Unremunerated Toil." In it Mark Twain claims that he had been reading an article in a French magazine about American humorists. The French author, according to Twain, says that Twain's story "The Jumping Frog" is a funny story, "but still he can't see why it should ever really convulse any one with laughter."[4] Then (according to Twain) the French author translates the whole story into French, so that his readers can see why it is not all that funny. Twain writes, "Just there is where my complaint originates. He has not translated it at all; he has simply mixed it all up; it is no more like the Jumping Frog when he gets through with it than I am like a meridian of longitude."[5] To prove the point, Twain claims he will now, in this book, print the original story again, then print the French translation, and then retranslate the French version back into English. Twain admits he cannot himself speak French, but, he protests, "I can translate very well, though not fast, I being self-educated."[6]

The story is less than a dozen pages in length. The French rendering (which begins a couple of pages into the story) is very good. Then follows Mark Twain's "retranslation." To give the flavor of the experiment, here are the first few lines of the original story to be translated.

> [W]ell, there was a feller here once by the name of Jim Smi-ley, in the winter of '49—or may be it was the spring of '50—I don't recollect exactly, somehow, though what makes me think it was one or the other is because I remember the big flume warn't finished when he first come to the camp; but any way, he was the curiosest man about always betting on any-thing that turned up you ever see, if he could get anybody to be on the other side; and if he couldn't he'd change sides.[7]

I shall spare you the French, but no French grammarian could criticize it. Here is Mark Twain's "retranslation":

> It there was one time here an individual known under the name of Jim Smiley: it was in the winter of '49, possibly well at the spring of '50, I no me recollect not exactly. This which me makes to believe that it was the one or the other, it is that I shall remember that the grand flume is not achieved when he arrives at the camp for the first time, but of all sides he was the man the most fond of to bet which one have seen, betting upon all that which is presented, when he could find an adversary; and when he not of it could not, he passed to the side opposed.[8]

And much more of the same. What Mark Twain has done, of course, is to translate the French literally. He has all the words "right"—properly spelled, with at least the lexical meaning right—but he has followed French word order, ignored matters of syntax and idiom, and blissfully refused to allow context to shape the pragmatic usage of a word. And then he blames the Frenchman for improperly translating! And that, of course, is what makes this piece so funny. (It is funnier yet if you read French well and can read the intermediate text.)

It reminds me of a letter my Dad received when he was a young man. At the time he was trying to plant an evangelical

Baptist church in French Canada. A well-meaning English-speaking Canadian from another part of the country wrote to him and said she would be willing to translate anything he gave her, because she had such a burden for the people Dad was trying to reach. She admitted she knew no French, but she was willing to look up every single word in an English-French dictionary, write down the equivalent, and render the English text into French. Of course, it cannot be done. For a start, English-French dictionaries do not provide just one option for any particular word, but many, and which option you choose turns on a myriad of factors. More important, the syntax and idioms of the two languages are so different that such an effort would produce something even funnier than Mark Twain. The spirit indeed was willing, but the *sarx* was ignorant.

Less Than the Text

Because no two languages share exactly the same structure and vocabulary (and a lot of other things), it is impossible not to lose something when you translate an extended text from one language to another.[9]

A couple of illustrations will make the point. Consider the absolute Greek expression *egō eimi*.[10] First-year Greek students will render this "I am." Second-year students will know that sometimes it should be translated "It is I" (or, in idiomatic American English, "It's me"), and that at other times it should be rendered "I am he" or the like, where the "he" is established by the context. In a famous passage, Jesus declares, "Before Abraham was, *egō eimi*" (John 8:58), which most of our translations rightly render "I am." The Jews he is confronting pick up stones to kill him, perceiving that he is speaking blasphemously. Not only does the link with Abraham entail the conclusion that Jesus is claiming preexistence, but this is the name of God. In Isaiah God declares, "I am he" (Isa. 41:4; 43:10), which in the Septuagint appears simply as *egō eimi*.

Unless you are reading the Greek text of John's Gospel, however, you may not realize that *ego eimi* has already occurred twice before in John 8. John 8:24 finds Jesus saying (in the NIV), "I told you that you would die in your sins; if you do not believe that *I am the one I claim to be,* you will indeed die in your sins." The NIV provides a footnote for the italicized words: Or *I am he.* Verse 28 is similar. The NRSV, NASB, and many others simply offer *I am he.*[11] Why not render it "I am"?

But that would be misleading. In the context, the entire debate concerns Jesus' identity. His opponents do not yet perceive that "I am" is what it transparently means in 8:58. At this stage, the Greek most naturally *means* "I am (the one I've been talking about)" or "I am (the one under discussion)" or "I am (he)" or the like.[12] To translate it absolutely, "I am," is not more "literal," it is merely more formal—and in this case the formal equivalence is positively misleading, for it is not what the Greek *means.* On the other hand, by the time the thoughtful reader of Greek has read through the entire chapter a few times, he or she cannot fail to remember, while reading John 8:58, the instances of *ego eimi* in John 8:24, 28. This thoughtful reader will recognize that the translations I have suggested above for verses 24 and 28 are necessary *as translations* but, knowing that John is a careful writer who repeatedly introduces a new term or theme that is unpacked only later in the book, will wonder whether *ego eimi* in 8:24, 28 is intentionally evocative. In other words, the competent reader of Greek, coming across John 8:24, 28 for the first time, reads *ego eimi* and does not connect it with the divine name. But after reading John 8:58 and the whole chapter several times, that reader will begin to wonder if the use of *ego eimi* in 8:24, 28 is *meant* to anticipate the end of the chapter and evoke what is clear by the time one reads 8:58. Incidentally, if some literalist argues, on formal grounds, that the only correct way to translate the Greek expression *ego eimi* is always to render it simply "I am," I insist that that person does not really understand Greek. The best proof, in this instance, is John 9:9, where the same words are not from the mouth of Jesus. The man born blind, now healed of his illness, must convince the skeptics that he really is the man who was formally blind. Some neighbors and others claim he is; the skeptics insist he only looks like him. "But he himself insisted, 'I am the man [*egō eimi*].'" Clearly, in this context the expression cannot be christological, and cannot be rendered "I am," but *means,* in English, "I am he," or, more idiomatically, "I am the man." That may be an English gloss, but in this context it is a correct English gloss.

All this is pretty clear to the person who thoughtfully and repeatedly reads John's Gospel in Greek. It is virtually impossible to pick up on these matters if you read John's Gospel in English. If you render *egō eimi* in 8:24, 28 as "I am" in order to preserve the connection with 8:58, you have overtranslated, indeed mistranslated, the expression. If instead you render it as does the NIV or NRSV in 8:24, 28, you are formally correct so far as Greek syntax is concerned in this context, but you have lost the evocative connection with verse 58. Either way, something is lost. And there are many, many examples of that sort of thing. That is one of the reasons, of course, why we still teach ministerial candidates to read the Greek and Hebrew texts. Translation is treason.

Again, consider Psalm 127:1, 3: "Unless the LORD builds the house, its *builders* labor in vain. Unless the LORD watches over the city, the watchmen stand guard in vain. . . . *Sons* are a heritage from the LORD, children a reward from him." It is well known that "house" in Hebrew can refer to either the dwelling or the family. But the English reader is unlikely to detect that this intended ambiguity is developed by Solomon, the psalmist, in the pun he employs: the word for "builders" is (in full diacritical transliteration) *bônîm,* and the word for "sons" is *bānîm.* There are many different kinds of wordplays in the Hebrew Bible, of course, and the overwhelming majority of them are lost in translation.[13] These are all instances where the translation provides, in certain respects, *less* than the text.

More Than the Text

On the other hand, it is easy to find instances where the translation, because of the differences between the donor language and the receptor language, necessarily says *more* than the text. We may restrict ourselves to a couple of examples.

Many languages around the world, especially in Africa, have an inclusive "we" and an exclusive "we." The use of "inclusive" in this case has nothing to do with gender. An inclusive "we" means the speaker *includes* the readers or hearers in the "we"; and exclusive "we" means the speaker *excludes* the readers or hearers from the "we." In such languages, every time the writer or speaker wants to say "we," he or she *must* choose one of these two forms: there is no other way of saying "we."

In a book like 1 John, "we" occurs frequently. Some of the references are contextually obvious: for example, the "we" in "we proclaim to you" (1 John 1:3) is obviously exclusive. But there are many examples where scholars are divided—as also in some of the "we" passages in Paul. But if you are translating the text into one of the languages where you *must* use either an inclusive we or an exclusive we, you *must* specify. There is no choice in the receptor language. Thus in the donor language, you may leave the matter unresolved, for in reality it is not specified by the form and may not be clear in the context. But in the receptor language, since you *must* make a choice, you force the text to be more specific than the donor text.

Similarly, a language without a passive voice often forces the translator to specify subjects that are not specified in the passive voice.

Context and Contexts

By now it should be clear that a word does not carry its lexical meaning(s)—that is, the meaning(s) one finds for that word in a lexicon—into each context where it is used. A lexicon of a dead language like Latin or Hellenistic Greek, after all, is nothing more than some scholar's attempt to classify the different meanings that a word appears to have in all its occurrences in a body of literature. To read all such meanings back into a particular usage is what is called "illegitimate totality transfer."

Two or three things follow from this. (1) Context is king. While there are other factors for establishing the meaning of a word in a particular text, the most important factor, by far, is a good understanding of the context. (2) Words shape their contexts, and the meanings of those words *in* their context are in turn shaped *by* their context. In other words, the meaning of a word in its context is not its lexical meaning (a more or less artificial construct) but is established by its interaction with its context, which includes syntactical elements, discourse elements, literary genre, semantic elements (that is, elements of meaning), and more.

We have already seen this to be so in the case of *sarx* ("flesh") and *lampros* ("bright"). Note how even the words I enclosed in quotation marks and parentheses are slightly misleading. It is not quite right to say that the Greek word "sarx" *means* "flesh." In certain contexts, as we have seen, it *means* something else. The word "flesh" is really the English "gloss" on the Greek word, but an English gloss should never be confused with the genius of what the word means within its own language, in its own varied contexts. The demands of translation require that we say the donor word "means" such and such in our receptor language, and that may be right in that context. It does not follow that the meaning of the word in the donor language is exactly the same as the meaning of the gloss word in the receptor language, for the overlap between two such words is almost never 100 percent.

That is why one cannot responsibly translate a text under some rigid dictum that the same word in the receptor language must always render a word in the donor text. This has been understood for centuries. The first English Bible, never printed, was the product of a group of scholars gathered around

John Wycliffe. It was a word-for-word rendering of the Latin, and almost unreadable. Just a few years after Wycliffe's death, however, in 1395 or 1396, John Purvey reworked the Wycliffe rendering to make it more readable in English. In his preface, Purvey writes, "First, it is to be known that the best translating out of Latin into English is to translate after the sentence and not only after the words. . . . The words ought to serve to the intent and sentence, or else the words be superfluous or false."[14] Similarly, in the preface to the 1611 edition of the King James Version, the translators confess, "We have not tied ourselves to a uniformity of phrasing or to an identity of words as some peradventure would wish that we had done." Of course they didn't: they were good communicators. So it is a bit frustrating, six centuries after Purvey and almost four centuries after the KJV, to find Robert Martin criticizing the NIV for not maintaining the same receptor terms for specific donor terms.[15] At the very least he might have evenhandedly treated the KJV to the same sanctions.

Other components of the "context" deserve mention. There is not only the immediate context, but a variety of more extended contexts. The immediate context may help an interpreter or a translator follow the flow of the argument more precisely, which may shed light on the coloring of a particular word or expression, which may affect translation choices. But there are expanding circles of larger contexts: the chapter, the book, the corpus, that period of literature (for example, one moves from some phrase in Romans 7 to all of chapter 7 to the entire Book of Romans to the Pauline corpus to the New Testament to Hellenistic Greek). Each "context" may make a contribution to understanding something small, even a word. For instance, the context of the corpus is important because individual authors use words differently. In other words, Paul does not simply write Greek, he writes his own "idiolect" of Greek. Demonstrably, he uses some words differently from the way other writers in the New Testament use them (for example, *kaleō*, "to call"). Nevertheless, the full range of Hellenistic Greek literature helps to establish how some vocabulary and some syntactical units mean something a little different from what they mean in Classical Greek. For instance, intensive forms of Greek verbs have often lost their intensiveness (but this can be determined only by inspection); the complex syntax of Greek conditionals in the Hellenistic period is nevertheless a good deal simpler than what prevails in the Classical period.

Moreover, one element in context is the literary genre in which an expression is found. These genres are not all transportable across linguistic lines. The French have nothing quite like a limerick; contemporary English has nothing quite like apocalyptic. The latter, for instance, delights in mixed metaphors. How much should such matters be explained in footnotes or by some other device, since they were part of the understood meaning that was both intended by the author and understood by the first readers?

Then there is the emotional overtone of certain expressions, whether of those expressions themselves, or when they are embedded in certain contexts. The German word *Schriftbeweis* has very positive overtones; something like "Scripture prooftext" as a rendering is a failure, not because at the level of naked meaning it is entirely wrong, but because the English expression usually carries negative overtones. In any case the German word is broader and subtler in meaning. In Acts 8:20, Peter says to Simon Magus (in the NIV), "May your money perish with you." An idiomatic rendering would be, "To hell with you and your money"—though of course it would be improper to render the Greek that way, because the English expression is customarily used in coarse and vulgar contexts today, thereby investing it with a tone absent from Peter's solemn words.

But there are still other kinds of context. Few have done more in this area than Ernst-August Gutt.[16] He points out how there may be more than the merely literary context at stake. The original text had not only a larger literary context but a social context. Perhaps I might offer an example other than his. In John 6, Jesus claims to be the bread from heaven, the bread of life.

In the literary context, there are connections with the bread that Jesus provided the day before at the feeding of the five thousand, and with the manna in the wilderness. But in addition to such explicit literary contextual features, there are implicit contextual features. One of these is that the words were first uttered in an agrarian society, among relatively poor people. For people in that society, bread was one of two staples; bread was something without which you died. Moreover, because the culture was agrarian, virtually everyone recognized, casually, that everything we eat is organic (save for a few minerals like salt): something dies, we eat it, and live. This is true whether we slaughter a pig and eat ham, or kill a stick of celery and eat it. Those living organisms die, so that we might live. Either they die, or we do. Thus when Jesus says that he is the bread of life, we ought to "hear" connections not only with the feeding of the five thousand and with the manna, but with the assumptions of the culture at that time. Jesus dies, we live; he is the staple of eternal life; without him and his death, we die.

There are many, many hundreds of such examples in the Bible.

Sociolinguistics and Culture

In recent years there has been a rising interest in examining how language and other cultural realities interact with each other. When you move into another language that is located in and forms part of a different culture, the interactions between language and culture are quite different. Keeping your eye on such matters is exceedingly difficult, but it is nevertheless part of the competent translator's responsibility.

There are a little over a dozen words in the Greek New Testament that might in some contexts be rendered "slave." The only one of these that must be rendered "slave," if we follow Greek precedent, is *doulos*. In the KJV, however, the vast majority of occurrences of *doulos,* especially when referring to believers, are rendered "servant." It is difficult to resist the supposition that "slave" seemed too harsh and unattractive, not least because of the social and cultural realities of the time. Modern translations rightly render far more occurrences as "slave" than did the KJV. Even there, however, some experts, rightly or wrongly, still prefer to retain "servant" in a few cases, because although they acknowledge that *doulos* in Greek settings always means "slave," they think that Hebrew *ᶜebed* ("servant") has influenced *doulos*. Certainly underlying Hebrew has modified some other Greek vocabulary. Whatever the outcome of that debate, it is hard to resist the conclusion that our renderings are influenced by our social contexts.

Moreover, both our language and our own social context change, and those changes may well call forth changes in translation. I have already offered a few instances of changes in English usage that have called forth more contemporary translation. Thirty years ago, "I have to buy a mouse" would conjure up a purchase for a child who wanted a pet in a little cage; now the same sentence conjures up a component for a computer system. So most of us are familiar with the reality that language changes, even though we may dispute how much it has changed. Part of the problem, as we shall see (chapter 9), is that America and many other Western countries are now so diverse that language that communicates well with one subgroup does not necessarily communicate well with another. What is at stake, in any case, is some sort of interchange between language and social context. But there are other changes in our social context that are still more revealing.

Consider, for example, Luke 17:34–35. The KJV reads, "I tell you, in that night there shall be two men in one bed; the one shall be taken, and the other shall be left. Two women shall be grinding together; the one shall be taken, and the other left." The Greek text includes neither the word "men" nor the word "women." In both cases, the Greek text simply reads, "there shall be two in one bed" / "Two shall be grinding together." In the culture of Jesus' day, if two were grinding together it was probably a hand mill, and the two were most likely women, even though the text does not say so. But why the KJV inserts the word "men" I cannot guess: earlier English versions had not done so, and I know of no reason to suppose that it was more common to have two men in one bed than two women or a man and a woman. The sex of the two individuals is not at issue in the context in any case; the point is that of two people who are in close relation, one is taken and the other is not. But in today's social context, two men in a bed hints at things the KJV translators would not have thought of (although certainly had they done so, they would not have approved). The words may be the same, but the social context of the readers has changed, resulting in different understandings of the same words. Most modern translations avoid the trap, either by following the Greek more closely (for example, the NRSV simply uses "two"), or by some other device (for example, "two people" / "two women," NLT). The NKJV maintains the KJV error. But my point is simply that social dynamics interact with language, both at the donor end and at the receptor end.

Finally, the combination of contexts contributes mightily to enabling language to *do* things. Language does not merely convey information (though of course it does that). Language commands, exhorts, entices; some passages evoke tears or wrath; they may set up models that implicitly invite imitation. Language *performs* things. Reflection on this reality has led to what is now commonly called "speech act theory." Ideally, a good translator wants to know not only what the donor text says but what it performs, that is, how it functions both in the literary context and among the readers for whom it was first intended. The translator will try to create a text in the receptor language that mirrors all of these components. The receptor text should, ideally, say what the donor text says (though for any sustained text a translation will *never* say it in exactly the same way), but it should also perform the same way, both in the literary context and among the readers to whom it is now being sent.[17]

Implications and Conclusions

In this chapter I have tried to avoid the issues of inclusive language. But issues of inclusive language are necessarily part of broader issues in translation theory and practice, and cannot receive an adequate evaluation without some knowledge of these broader issues.

1. While avoiding the use of too many technical terms, the preceding discussion has introduced some important categories in linguistics and translation theory. By now it should be clearer why the Italian proverb is important: translation *is* treason. No translation is perfect.

2. This does not mean that there are not better and worse translations. But even the scales on which "better" and "worse" are measured are tricky things. One might have a Bible translation that is "better" than many others in the general faithfulness of its renderings but uses vocabulary that is large and elevated, with the result that it is "worse" in its ability to serve the masses (so, for instance, the REB). One might have a translation that is wonderfully effective in its ability to communicate and thus be a "better" translation, but at the expense of too little faithfulness, too many clichés in the receptor language, too much loss of the more subtle elements of the donor language, and thus be a "worse" translation.

3. The challenges in translation that this chapter has briefly mentioned (and there are many, many more) do not mean that there are some things that *cannot* be translated. Although there are a few philosophers of language who claim this is the case (thus taking "translation is treason" to an extreme), the overwhelming majority of linguists and translators insist, rightly in my view, that any element in any text can be translated, except for some forms.[18] *But they cannot all be translated in the same way and in the same limited space as in the donor text.* Sometimes the only way something can be adequately explained in the receptor language is by an explanatory note. Translators make choices: lose some of the Greek passives in

order to make the text sound like smooth English, specify whether the "we" is inclusive or exclusive to accommodate Kikuyu syntax (even though the donor text makes no such specification), and so forth.

In one of the more interesting experiments to come along, the NET Bible offers not only explanatory notes but also very extensive "translator's notes."[19] The notes are about five times the length of the biblical text. Whether or not one agrees with individual translation choices, at the very least the perusal of such notes helps the novice identify the plethora of choices that the translator is constantly called to make and some of the reasons for deciding this way or that way. Although translations may be better or worse, it is crucial to remember that translation is not an exact science.

4. Translation is inevitable. Human beings made in the image of God will communicate with one another. Moreover we who have a revelation from God in words, and a commission to make that revelation known, must be at the forefront of thinking through the challenges and possibilities of translation.

5. The commonly mooted contrast between "literal" and "paraphrastic" translations is not very helpful or insightful, partly because most who use this polarity associate "literal" with superior or faithful or exact, and "paraphrastic" with shoddy or slippery or approximate. But sometimes, as we have seen, a formally more *literal* rendering may be *less* accurate, because of the differences between the two languages. It may be better to create a spectrum from "more formal translations" to "more fluid translations" or "more functional translations," or something of that sort, because there is less emotional baggage associated with such expressions. No translation is exclusively formal;[20] none entirely avoids formal features. If I were placing some contemporary versions on this sliding scale, the arrangement might look like this:

ASV NASB KJV NKJV RSV NRSV NJB NIV NIVI NLT CEV LB

Nor is it simply a question of word-for-word translations over against phrase-for-phrase translations, or even thought-for-thought translations. As we have seen, there are entire phrases in Greek and Hebrew that have no precise parallels in English, just as there are words in Greek and Hebrew that have no precise parallels in English. One understands what people are trying to say when they speak of a "thought-for-thought" translation, but quite frankly the expression is misleading. There are no thoughts to be translated apart from the expression of such thoughts in words, phrases, clauses, sentences, text. In practice, "thought-for-thought" translation can easily become an excuse for finding the general "thought" of a passage and paraphrasing it, without closely trying to "hear" *all* the thoughts that are bound up in a text, reflected in *all* the words in this particular syntax, discourse, genre, and so on, and trying to render as many of them as possible in the receptor language in comparable space. *All* translations, from the most formal to the most functional, are mediated by thought: the translators think they understand the thoughts that are being conveyed, and try to convey them in the receptor language.

6. In the same way, debates about the merits of one translation theory over against another are sometimes fraught with approval and disapproval without any real understanding of the issues involved. None of the so-called translation theories is disjunctively set over against all the other translation theories; they, too, are *necessarily* placed on a kind of spectrum, or at least within the same sphere. For example, "formal equivalence" theory is often contrasted with "dynamic equivalence" theory. One can find voices that praise one and condemn the other. But just as it is easy to read both theories sympathetically, so also is it easy to mock both theories. For reasons we have already seen, consistent execution of formal equivalence is impossible, and if one opts for the axiom "as formal as possible," one frequently ends up with a translation that actually distorts much of the meaning in the donor text. On the other hand, when dynamic equivalence theory was first formulated and pro-

moted, it emphasized the importance of producing a receptor text that achieved the same results among its readers as the donor text achieved among its readers. The intention was good, but the formulation slightly silly: in most instances we have very little information about how ancient texts were received. And even if we did, the criterion is not necessarily helpful, as sometimes texts were received very badly (for example, not everyone in Corinth was happy with all of Paul's letters!), owing less to the words themselves than to the unpopularity, in that theological and social context, of the message they conveyed. For this and other reasons, virtually no one in the field of Bible translation uses the expression "dynamic equivalence" anymore: since 1986 it has been displaced by "functional equivalence."[21] Those who continue to use it are almost invariably opponents of anything but formal equivalence theory, and for them "dynamic equivalence" is a form of opprobrium.

In some circles this debate has been eclipsed. In an important series of books and articles, Ernst-August Gutt has argued for "relevance theory" in translation.[22] In a nutshell, relevance theory stipulates that the ultimate (but not the only) test of a translation is whether or not it achieves with the target audience what the translator sets out to achieve. Obviously there is considerable insight here. What the translators of the LB or NLT set out to achieve is not what the translators of the RSV or NIV set out to achieve, so in certain respects they have to be measured by different criteria. But in the hands of reductionists, relevance theory in Bible translation could easily fail to reflect adequately on the translator's responsibility toward the donor text, as well as his or her responsibility toward the target audience.

7. By now it should be obvious that no translation is accomplished without interpretation. This needs unpacking a little. For some people, "interpretation" is a negative word. They have heard it too often in expressions like "That's just your interpretation" or "My interpretation is as good as your interpretation" or the like. For them, "interpretation" represents

distance from the text. What they want is simply the text. The translator's task is to render the text, not some interpretation of it.

At one level, one must respect their concern to be faithful to the text, their theoretical commitment not to play fast and loose with it. Doubtless their sensitivity to such matters has been increased by the insistence of some postmoderns that meaning resides in interpreters and not in the text. But in reality, every reading of a text by a finite being is an interpretation of it. There are more faithful interpretations and less faithful interpretations, more accurate interpretations and less accurate interpretations, but we cannot avoid interpretations.[23]

So when I say that *no* translation is accomplished without interpretation, I am saying nothing more than that translation is never a merely mechanical task divorced from interpretation.[24] Precisely because there are differences between the donor and receptor languages, it is impossible simply to provide formal equivalents. Translators must *understand* the donor text, or think they do, before rendering it into the receptor text. This does not mean that every alleged "understanding" of a text is as good as any other, or that translators enjoy a sovereign freedom from the responsibility to improve and hone and correct their understandings of the text. It does mean that criticism of a particular translation because it is based on an interpretation of a text is silly, because that could be said of every translation. If one wishes to criticize a translation because of the interpretation that undergirds it, one must rather say that the interpretation is faulty for such-and-such reasons, and provide a superior interpretation. Every translation reflects a reading of the text; every Bible translation reflects a theological reading of the text.

8. All translations are temporary. This is because the receptor language changes; there are no exceptions. This means that those responsible for a certain translation have only three options. *(a)* When a translation is completed and is circulating, they can disband. That translation may continue in print

indefinitely. But eventually, whether in twenty years or four centuries, its market share and influence will decline, as that version is eclipsed by others that are geared to the most recent developments in the language. *(b)* Those responsible may elect to introduce a major revision every forty, fifty, or one hundred years. Thus both the RSV and NASB build off the ASV; the NRSV builds off the RSV; the NLT builds off the LB; the REB builds off the NEB; and so forth. Inevitably, however, these "revisions" become in effect new versions, precisely because they are sufficiently different from those that undergird them that both can usefully be kept in print, the older version gradually losing its influence to the more recent version. This is not necessarily a bad option. Nevertheless, it must be understood that each major revision of an English version, even when it is based on the original languages, is a version *within a certain tradition* of a translation. It is not "fresh." Moreover, it has sectioned the market once again by providing further options. *(c)* Those responsible for the translation may establish a committee that makes incremental changes every few years and publish only the most recent revision. That happened at first in an ad hoc fashion to the KJV until its text was finally firm. The approach of IBS toward the NIV was more programmatic. The New Testament was lightly revised when it first appeared with the Old Testament. The entire NIV was lightly revised again in 1984. The advantage of such a procedure is that the worst errors can be removed, and the translation is more likely to remain contemporary, and therefore useful to the church, for a longer period than it otherwise would. When publishers make these incremental changes, they let the older versions lapse, precisely because the aim of the exercise is to keep this "renewed" version contemporary. But there are disadvantages and dangers. If the responsible body introduces changes too often, at any given time there will be two or more editions of a version in circulation (even if the publisher is not producing any more of the older ones), and this inhibits corporate reading and liturgical use (though not private reading). Moreover, if the version becomes very popular (like the NIV), and if the responsible body then introduces more than minor changes, there may be a hue and cry of the "Hands off my NIV!" sort. This cry may be theologically driven; it may be nothing more than rank traditionalism; it may be some combination of both. If the publishers agree to make *no* more changes, then the version (in this case, the NIV) is locked in time, and we have tumbled into the first option. The version will eventually be eclipsed. Of course, in due course the publishers could opt for a major revision and a new name while keeping the current NIV in print: in other words, they could pursue option *b,* providing, say, the RNIV (Revised New International Version), keeping both NIV and RNIV in print. What that means is that in the passage of time the NIV itself will eventually lose its dominance and be largely replaced by other versions, the RNIV or others (which may or may not be superior—or, more realistically, will be superior in some ways and inferior in others). In short, those who are insisting that IBS and Zondervan make *no* more revisions to the NIV, including the kinds of revisions that might generate a "new" version (such as my mythical RNIV), are demanding that these organizations commit themselves to option *a.*

My suspicion is that at least some spokespersons who said they hoped that eventually NIVI would displace the NIV did so because they knew that up until now IBS and Zondervan had thought of handling the NIV within option *c.* No one is keeping the 1978 edition in print. In this case, however, the changes are sufficiently substantial that, whether you like them or not, they are widely perceived as constituting a new version, rather than a new edition of an old version. If IBS and Zondervan, responding to the crisis, are genuinely committed to keeping the NIV in print *as it is,* then they have shut down option *c* and have only the other two.[25]

9. In this chapter I have tried to get across some basic principles of linguistics and translation theory without indulging in too many technicalities or succumbing to too much tech-

nical vocabulary. One technical term that did creep in was "gloss." I shall close by reflecting on its significance for our subject, and by briefly introducing two more terms.

Very often Greek lexica provide some sort of awkward combination of meanings and glosses, and linguistically uninformed readers confuse the two. Ideally a Greek lexicon (for example) should provide as accurate a picture as possible of the meaning(s) of the word within the structure and semantics of the Greek language. Of course, if it is a Greek-English lexicon, it must do so in English. That is the problem. Very often what a lexicon provides is not quite the *meaning* of the word in a particular context *in Greek* (explained in English), but merely a useful translation equivalent, a "gloss," the appropriate word for the English translation because that is the way we say it. We shall soon see that confusion between "meaning" and "gloss" bedevils not a little of the contemporary debate over inclusive-language translations.

A second confusion may as well be mentioned now, as it will become important later. A crucial distinction must be made between "meaning" and "referent." The "meaning" of a word is its sense.[26] We may then distinguish, for example, between lexical meaning (that is, the more-or-less analytic and sometimes synthetic sense assigned a word in a lexicon) and pragmatic meaning (that is, what sense it carries in a particular context). The "referent" of a word is what it is referring to. Some words have only meaning: for example, "a" and "beautiful." Some words are only referential, especially proper names: for example, "Paul" *refers* to a man called Paul. Some proper names, of course, while referring to someone or something, also have meaning, either directly or as some kind of pun (for example, Moses and Abraham).[27] Some words have meaning and are usually nonreferential but may become referential in certain contexts: for example, "twelve" is not usually referential, but if substantivized in the right context, "the Twelve" might *refer* to the twelve apostles. The distinction between meaning and referent will become critical later in this book.

Until the last few paragraphs, this chapter has made little mention of the debate that this book is trying to address. Some knowledge of the challenging work of translation is helpful in discussing the peculiar challenge of gender-related questions. Similarly, some grasp of the nature of gender in various languages around the world will occupy most of our attention in the next chapter, before we return, at the end of the chapter, to a brief consideration of gender questions in the Bible.

4

GENDER AND SEX AROUND THE WORLD

A TRANSLATOR'S NIGHTMARE

Most of this chapter, like the previous one, will avoid saying much about the English language or about translation of the Bible into English, until the last couple of sections. For just as it is important to reflect on the nature of language before we can say much that is very penetrating about translation from language to language, so it is important to reflect on the nature of gender in language before we deal with the translation of gender from one language to another.

I must say at once that in this chapter I am enormously indebted to Dr. Norman Fraser, who has picked me up on matters linguistic in the past, and who kindly responded to my e-mail asking for information with an informed bibliography (which I have dutifully read) and his own voluminous notes. These I have cribbed shamelessly (though I have tried to check them out for myself in the sources).

Grammatical Gender

Preliminary Matters

In the literature of sociologists and of feminists and their opponents, sex is a matter of biology while gender is a matter of social construction.[1] Almost without exception, linguists look at the matter differently. For them, gender is a grammatical category, while sex is a semantic category (a category of meaning). True, there is some kind of connection between grammatical gender and the sex of the referent: gender and sex clearly interact. But the nature of this interaction varies enormously from language to language. To take an easy example, when French classifies the word "table" as feminine, nothing is being said about the sex of the table. In fact, in languages around the world, the number of grammatical genders in the different gender systems varies from two to about thirty, and so far as I know there are not thirty sexes. In most languages that employ strong gender systems, the primary purpose of gender is not to encode sex but to encode agreement among elements in the sentence. This is more difficult to perceive in English than in some languages, but I hope the point will become clear over the next few pages.

Gender Systems: Their Distribution and Variations

The category of gender is not found in every language. Most (but not all) of the Indo-European languages (to which group both Greek and English belong) have it, usually with two or three genders. Most of the major Asian languages do not have gender; the Dravidian languages constitute an exception. The Caucasian languages have gender systems that are usually more complex than those in Indo-European languages and are rather differently structured. Languages change with time, of course, and may modify their gender systems. The Slavonic languages are currently spawning new "subgenders," owing to the fact that some other category such as animacy interacts with gender to create new agreement patterns. There are four language groups (comprising about nine hundred languages) in Africa. Afro-Asiatic languages usually have two-gender systems. The other three groups, Nilo-Saharan, Niger-Kordofanian, and Khoisan, all include languages with gender systems, though not every language in these groups uses gender systems (experts estimate that about two-thirds of Africa's nine hundred languages have some form of gender system). A majority of the more than eight hundred languages of New Guinea have gender systems. Gender is also prevalent in the languages of Australia, especially in Arnhem Land and the North Kimberleys. By contrast, gender is relatively uncommon in the languages of the Americas, except for the Algonquian family.

Gender specification normally demands some sort of agreement with other elements in the sentence. Even first-year Greek students understand this point, but let me try to explain it for those whose only tongue is English. Consider the three expressions "a wise woman," "a wise man," "some wise women." In English, the modifying adjective "wise" has exactly the same form in all three expressions. In many languages, however, the word "wise" would have to be spelled a little differently in the three expressions: it would have to *agree* grammatically with the word that it modifies. If the word is grammatically feminine, then "wise" would have to be feminine; if masculine, then "wise" would have to be masculine; if feminine plural, then "wise" would have to be feminine plural. But some languages have forms for plural regardless of gender: in that case we say that the adjective is marked for number but not for gender. In such a language, "wise" would be spelled the same way in the expression "some wise men" and "some wise women." In any case, languages with gender systems normally demand gender agreement between related words.

Turning to the nouns, clearly "woman" in English is marked for number: the singular form is distinguished from the plural "women" by a change in spelling. Note, too, that English has two articles. The definite article "the" is not marked for number: one can say "the wise woman" and "the wise women," and the word "the" remains the same. But in English the indefinite article "a" is singular: we say "a wise woman" but we cannot say "a wise women." Where forms are marked for number, once again agreement must normally be achieved.[2] So gender systems must normally be in agreement, and number systems must normally be in agreement—as also case systems, which I briefly illustrated in chapter 3 (point 3 under "Differences from Language to Language").

Agreement may be expressed in a number of ways. Very commonly it is expressed through "inflection": that is, the words that must "agree" with one another change their endings ("suffixes"), beginnings ("prefixes"), or something in the middle ("infixes"), or some combination of all three. Thus in Greek, for instance, in the expression "the glorious truth" all three words—the article, the adjective, and the noun—must agree in number (in this example, singular), gender (feminine, because "truth" is feminine in Greek), and case (which will be determined by the use to which the expression is put in its syntactical location). Agreement may also be reflected in the form of pronouns that have a gender-specific antecedent: for example, in English, "Mary combed *her* hair." Languages in which gender agreement manifests itself exclusively or almost exclusively among the pronouns are said to have pronominal gender systems. English is such a language; Hebrew and Greek are not.

How, then, are nouns assigned to genders? What makes "table" in French and "truth" in Greek feminine? The assignment can be made on (1) a semantic basis, that is, based on the meaning of words; (2) a formal basis, that is, regardless of the meaning, all nouns with a particular ending belong to specific gender; (3) some combination of the two. The experts say that every language with a gender system retains a semantic assignment for at least some words. When I specify a semantic basis (that is, a basis in the meaning of the words), this may or may not be sex-differentiating.

We need a couple of easy examples. In German, the word
Frau[3] can mean "woman" or "wife" or "Mrs." The word is
feminine, so the definite article in German (in the nominative case) must be *die: die Frau.* But one of the German
words for a young woman is *Mädchen.* This word is neuter,
because it has the diminutive ending *-chen,* which is always
neuter. The article with it must therefore be the neuter article: *das Mädchen.* In the first of these two nouns, the assignment of the word to a gender is tied to semantics, that is, to
the meaning of the word: "woman" or "wife" is feminine,
and so is the word *Frau.* In the second instance, the assignment of the word to a particular gender is tied to formal
requirements, regardless of the semantics: the formal
requirement is that words ending in *-chen* be neuter, regardless of their meaning.

In the list that follows, each entry begins with the name of
a language, followed by the family of languages to which it
belongs (in parentheses), followed by the number of genders
it has. The meaning of these genders is then listed. In other
words, in these languages we are dealing with semantic assignments (that is, nouns are assigned to genders on the basis of
meaning), though we shall quickly see that some of these
meanings are not sex-differentiating.

Tamil (Dravidian), 3
  1. male rational
  2. female rational
  3. nonrational—and as in many languages, infants are not
     rational, but the gods are, and so are some domestic pets
Parji (Dravidian), 2
  1. male
  2. nonmale (note: nonmale, not necessarily female)
Diyari (Australian), 2
  1. female, whether human or animal (in sex-differentiat-
     ing animals)
  2. nonfemale (note: nonfemale, not necessarily male)

Halkomelem (Salish), 2
1. females and diminutives
2. all others (hereafter referred to as "residue," the term commonly employed by linguists for "all the others")

Zande (Ubangian), 4
1. male human
2. female human
3. other animate
4. residue

Dyirbal (Australian, Northeast Queensland), 4
1. male human, nonhuman animate
2. female human, water, fire, fighting
3. nonflesh food
4. residue

Ojibwa (Algonquian), 2
1. animate, including trees
2. inanimate

Northern Cheyenne (Algonquian), 2
1. powerful things (with power defined, of course, according to the Cheyenne worldview)
2. residue

Tabasaran (Caucasian), 2
1. human
2. nonhuman

Lak (Caucasian), 4
1. male rational
2. female rational
3. other animate—but including some female humans and many inanimates
4. residue

Archi (Northeast Caucasian), 4
1. male rational
2. female rational
3. large things
4. small things and abstracts

Ngangikurrunggur (Daly, North Australian), 9
1. most natural objects, terms for kinship, a few body parts
2. hunting weapons
3. most body parts
4. trees, most wooden implements
5. most animals hunted for meat
6. edible plants
7. male animates, excluding dogs
8. female animates
9. canines

Ket (Siberian language isolate), 3
1. male human, male animal, some other living things, fish (with three exceptions), all growing trees, large wooden objects, the moon, some religious items
2. female human, female animal, other living things, three fish (turbot, ruff, perch), some plants, the sun, fire, some religious items, soul, some body parts, some skin diseases
3. parts of wholes, residue (actually the majority of Ket nouns)

Many languages, however, assign nouns on a formal basis (though some sort of semantic component is factored in). These languages are much more common than those with gender systems that assign nouns on a purely semantic basis (like those listed above). Moreover, not only do they vary enormously in complexity, but the nature of the formal characteristics according to which nouns are assigned gender can vary. Roughly speaking, formal characteristics may be divided into two divisions. Some assignments are made on the basis of *morphology,* that is, on the shape of words, commonly (but not invariably) realized in their endings; other assignments are made on the basis of *phonology,* that is, the way the word sounds. (Obviously these two are related, but not always strictly related; sometimes morphology takes precedence over phonology, and sometimes the reverse.)

Let us begin with languages that assign nouns to gender according to morphology. Even these languages have some semantic component. For example, in Russian (whose gender system has three genders), nouns that are sex-differentiable first of all follow these rules:[4]

1. nouns denoting males are masculine
2. nouns denoting females are feminine

Nouns that are not assigned according to these two rules fall into two categories: either they are declinable (that is, they fall into different patterns, called *declensions,* each with its own morphology) or they are indeclinable. For declinable nouns:

1. nouns of the first declension are masculine
2. nouns of the second and third declensions are feminine
3. nouns of the fourth declension are neuter

For indeclinable nouns:

1. nouns denoting animates are masculine
2. the residue are neuter

Other languages assign nouns to gender according to some phonological pattern, that is, according to the way words sound. For instance, Qafar (belonging to the East Cushitic family) has two genders. The first includes nouns denoting female humans and animals (a semantic assignment) and nouns whose lexical form ends in an accented vowel (a phonological assignment); the second embraces the residue. Hausa, an African language belonging to the Chadic family, also has two genders. The semantics are the same as in Qafar, but in addition nouns ending in *-aa* are feminine.

Some languages have resisted analysis until very recently. The gender system in French, for example, has often been judged to be arbitrary. It is now recognized that there are a couple of semantic assignment rules (sex-differentiable nouns denoting males are masculine; sex-differentiable nouns denoting females are feminine), a small number of morphological assignment rules (for example, compound nouns formed from a verb plus some other element are masculine), and a substantial number of phonological rules dealing with the final segment of words as they used to be pronounced in older French. In other words, one reason why French resisted analysis for so long is that the assignment of gender to nouns took place when many nouns, especially feminine nouns, were pronounced (and often spelled) a little differently from the way they are pronounced today.[5]

To add to the challenges, the gender systems in some languages are partly "syncretic," that is, different agreements are signaled by the same marker. For example, in Qafar, feminine singular verbs, masculine plural verbs, and feminine plural verbs all share the same *t*. In the Somali definite article, the masculine singular form and the feminine plural form are identical, while the feminine singular and the masculine plural forms are identical.

Agreement Patterns in Difficult Cases

In gender-marked languages, many agreements are straightforward, but inevitably difficulties of one sort or another arise.

One difficulty is how to sort out agreement between elements in the sentence that are gender-marked and elements that are not gender-marked (which linguists call "nonprototypical controllers"). Suppose English were a highly gender-marked language in its nouns and finite verbs. In the sentence "To err is human," the verb "is" would have some gender marker, and it should agree not only with "human" but also with the infinitive "to err." Unfortunately, the infinitive "to err" is not gender-marked. So what gender should be assigned to "is" and "human"?

Languages tend to resolve this problem in one of two ways. Some simply select one of the existing genders and assign it to tasks like this. Often enough it is the "residue" gender. In the following list, once again the language is followed by the family to which it belongs, and the number of genders in its gender system, followed by a list of those genders, with that gender in boldface type that is used for "neutral agreement," that is, for agreement with "nonprototypical controllers."

Serbo-Croat (South Slavonic), 3	masculine, feminine, **neuter**
Menominee (Algonquian), 2	animate, **inanimate**
Fula (West Atlantic), about 20	**the "Dum" class (most abstracts)**, about 19 others
Bayso (East Cushitic), 2	**masculine**, feminine
Qafar (East Cushitic), 2	masculine, **feminine**

The other way for languages to solve this problem is to generate a unique "neutral" (not neuter!) form that serves no purpose other than to solve this and related problems. For example, Spanish, like French but unlike German, has only two genders, masculine and feminine. But in addition to the masculine pronoun *el* and the feminine pronoun *ella*, it also has a neutral pronoun *ello*, which has no nouns that could serve as its normal antecedent but which solves the problem of "nonprototypical controllers." Portuguese has a similar arrangement. Ukranian (East Slavonic) has adjectival forms in *-o* for neutral agreement in predicative constructions.

A second problem that arises is what to do in gender-marked languages with masculine and feminine forms that are normally tied to the sex of the referent (male and female), but where the sex of the referent in some particular context is unknown. Four different strategies are used:

1. Use a regular form by convention. This may be:
    masculine: this is the majority pattern; for example, Serbo-Croat

feminine: this is the pattern adopted by a substantial minority of languages; for example, Maasai (Nilotic), Seneca (Iroquoian), Goajiro (Arawakan), Dama (Khoisan).

2. Use an evasive form. Some uses of "they" in English fall into this category. Polish employs its neuter form at this juncture. Archi (Caucasian) employs the form of its fourth gender structure—a gender that does not include nouns denoting humans!

3. Use a special form. If the gender of the referent is unknown, Zande (Ubangian) uses a special pronoun *ni* that is separate from the normal pronouns. Some uses of *on* in French and *man* in German approximate this.[6]

4. Follow no rule; decide on the spot. Dyirbal (Northeast Queensland) allows speakers to please themselves: if the sex of the referent is unknown, pick a gender, any gender.

A third problem that arises in gender-marked languages is what to do when there are gender conflicts. Consider the sentence, "When John and Susan visited the city, they went to see *Les Misérables*." In a gender-marked language, what gender should the pronoun "they" be (and with it the verb "went," if it too is marked)? After all, one of the nouns in the compound subject that constitutes the referent of "they" is masculine ("John"), and the other is feminine ("Susan"). What gender should "they" be?

Languages tend to adopt one of three solutions. They seek to resolve gender conflicts in coordinate structures on the basis of semantics (that is, meaning), on the basis of syntax, or on the basis of some combination of the two.

1. Semantic resolution: for example,
    Tamil (with only two genders in the plural):
    a. if all conjuncts[7] denote rationals, use the rational form

    b. if all conjuncts denote nonrationals, use the neuter form

    c. otherwise use the rational plural

   Archi (with four genders [see point 2 above]):

    a. if there is at least one conjunct denoting a rational, use gender 1 or 2

    b. otherwise use gender 3 or 4

   Luganda, a Bantu language (eight genders):

    a. if all conjuncts are human, use gender 1 or 2

    b. if none of the conjuncts is human, use gender 7 or 8

    c. otherwise use a comitative construction (that is, break the construction up) to avoid the problem; if it cannot be avoided, use gender 7 or 8

2. Syntactic resolution: for example,

   French (only two genders):

    a. if all conjuncts are feminine (regardless of meaning), use the feminine form

    b. otherwise use the masculine form

   Icelandic (three genders):

    a. if all conjuncts are masculine, use the masculine gender

    b. if all conjuncts are feminine, use the feminine gender

    c. otherwise use the neuter gender

3. Mixed semantic and syntactic resolution: for example,

   Latin (three genders)

    a. if all conjuncts are masculine, use the masculine gender

    b. if all conjuncts are feminine, use the feminine gender

    c. if all conjuncts denote humans, use the masculine gender

    d. otherwise use the neuter gender

Rumanian (three genders)
a. if at least one conjunct denotes a male animate, use the masculine gender
b. if all conjuncts are masculine, use the masculine gender
c. otherwise use the feminine gender

Gender and Translation

Some Reflections

One might well ask why so much space should be devoted to languages that are a long way removed from anything to do with gender-neutral English. Not for a moment am I suggesting that the move from Hebrew to English is encumbered with all the challenges implicit in the languages to which I have briefly referred. But I could not think of a better way of getting across a number of points that have an enormous bearing on the problem of translating (grammatical) gender. Not all of these points are directly applicable to English translations of Holy Scripture, but quite a few of them are.

So here are a few observations that largely spring from what has already been laid out in this chapter, sometimes moving toward fresh information. This list is not exhaustive of the lessons that should be learned, but it is representative and suggestive, and will advance the argument another step.

First, linguistic gender is a highly diverse phenomenon. A majority of languages have it, but many do not. Those that do have some gender system or other rarely have a gender system exactly like that in another language. The number, meaning, form, and use of genders are all highly variable. So also are the conventions for resolving gender conflicts, and for handling "non-prototypical controllers." The relation between grammatical gender and the sex of referents is also extremely variable. It does not take much imagination to discern how difficult a translator's job would be to render a Latin text into an Australian language, or into Qafar, or into one of the East Cushitic languages. In every case, something would be lost (apart from detailed footnotes), and in many cases the receptor language would have to over-specify. There simply is no choice; that is the nature of translation, and many of the challenges of translation are seen in an acute form in the area of grammatical gender.

Second, languages change with time, and that includes changes in gender systems. I briefly mentioned the changes currently taking place in Slavonic languages. In fact, there is a substantial literature on the rise, development, and decline of gender systems in various language families.[8] At the level of syntax, when languages simplify with time, such simplification tends to be matched by rising complexity elsewhere, such as in the morphology. But the opposite may happen: simplified morphology may be accompanied by a syntax of rising complexity, since every language has to encode its structural relations in one fashion or another. In morphology, Hellenistic Greek is simpler than Attic Greek; modern Greek is much simpler than Hellenistic Greek (for example, the genitive and dative have virtually disappeared). The main varieties of Chinese (Cantonese and Mandarin) are morphologically very simple (as is English), and their syntax and word order are correspondingly more complex.[9] But languages change, whether we like it or not. We may legitimately dispute how quickly English is changing: I'll say a little more about that below and considerably more in chapter 9. But change they will, including their gender systems, and translations will change with them.

Third, the function of gender systems is another extraordinarily variable element. As we have seen, gender systems establish agreement; in many cases, they carry semantic freight. But when one asks more pointedly why languages have gender systems (remembering, of course, that some languages do not), the answers are complex. In some instances, gender systems help to "disambiguate" the syntax, that is, to make sentences less ambiguous than they would otherwise be. Certain examples crop up in several reference works.[10] "Maria photographed Tobias in front of the house when *she/he/it* was ten years old." In this case, the choice of pronoun—feminine singular, masculine singular, or neuter singular—establishes the referent (Maria, Tobias, house) and therefore what it is that is ten years old. In languages where every noun is marked for gender, this may be of much greater importance than a language like English that is not so marked. Consider the German sentence, "Der Krug fiel in die Schale, aber er zerbrach nicht": "The jug fell in the bowl but *it* did not break." What did not break—the jug or the bowl? In German the answer is unambiguous, because the pronoun "er" is masculine, and agrees with "Krug" (jug) but not with "Schale" (bowl). Thus the German gender system "disambiguates" this particular structure where the nouns at issue are of different gender. But obviously if the two nouns were of the same gender, the gender system would not disambiguate the sentence.

In fact, the function of gender systems in different languages varies enormously. In some Australian languages, the gender system holds together much of the syntax. In other languages, gender systems may show the attitude of the speaker, or mark status, or display affection. In some Polish dialects, the feminine gender is used for women who are married (a status); neuter or masculine forms (depending on the dialect) are used for women who are unmarried. In some languages, affection is shown children by shifting genders—masculine for the girl, feminine for the boy. In some languages, people are referred to in nonanimate genders when they are being insulted.[11]

Fourth, English, as we have seen, has a pronominal gender system. Inevitably, many of our most difficult problems of gender resolution are connected with our pronouns. In contemporary English, the first-person singular pronoun "I" is not marked for gender, but it is marked for number (that is, it is distinguished from "we," but neither "I" nor "we" specifies a particular gender). The second-person pronoun "you" is marked for neither gender nor number—though of course older English distinguished the second-person pronoun for number and sometimes case: "thou" was second-person singular, nominative case, and "thee" was accusative case; the corresponding plurals were "ye" and "you." None of these pronouns is marked for gender. In the third person, the singular forms are marked for gender ("he," "she," "it"), but the plural form is not ("they").

Thus English has no third-person singular common-gender pronoun. The problem has been discussed at least since the eighteenth century; it is not the preserve of the past two or three decades (see discussion in chapter 9). Consider:

1. Everyone loves to hear his own name.
2. Everyone loves to hear her own name.
3. Everyone loves to hear his or her own name.
4. Everyone loves to hear their own name.

Most language authorities vote for the first option, and claim that in this case "his" is gender neutral, or common gender. Formally, of course, it is not, which is why some have advocated alternating between the first two options (a procedure adopted in some Australian languages), others head for the third option (which, strictly speaking, is the only one that follows formal agreement to the letter, but is usually viewed as too cumbersome), and still others choose the last option (which breaches concord of number). So the first option breaches concord of gender (or we avoid admitting this point by saying that "his" is gender neutral), while the last option breaches concord of number (and we avoid admitting this point by saying, as some do, that this "they" is singular).

Certainly the majority view, among competent authorities, until recently, was the first option; what the majority view is today is more difficult to determine, as we shall see. But we should observe that whatever one's view, one is forced by custom to choose the fourth option in certain constructions. For instance, one may say, "Everyone liked his dinner" (first option), but no one would say, "Everyone liked the dinner, but he did not care for the dessert." English usage dictates, rather, "Everyone liked the dinner, but they did not care for the dessert."[12] Why this exception should be made in standard English is dictated solely by usage. If usage changes (at least in some segments of the English-speaking world), it is difficult to see why the same singular "they" might not be used elsewhere, however much it may grate upon my purist sensibilities. When I was a child, "It is I" was still mandated; now most authorities sanction "It's me." This, too, grates on my purist sensibilities—but the changing usage is quite capable of breaching formal concord.

Fifth, from a translator's point of view, then, one must understand how the gender system works in both the donor language and the receptor language (assuming that both languages have such a system). The way affection is expressed to a child, for instance, may be entirely different in another language, with the loss of *formal* equivalence in gender in the receptor language in order to approximate the emotion of affection carried by the gender structures of the donor language. No two languages are mirror reflections of each other, even in their gender systems.

An Example

Rodney Venberg provides us with an interesting example of a translation problem that turns on gender.[13] Serving as a missionary translator with the Lutheran Brethren Mission in the Chad Republic, he devoted himself to learning the language of the Pévé tribe. The word for "God" in Pévé is *Ifray,* a feminine word. In Pévé legends, *Ifray* gave birth to two children, a boy and a girl, from whom the tribe descended. Using a feminine word for God is not in itself a problem, of course; the word for "spirit" in Hebrew is (normally) feminine. But quite apart from the lingering tribal traditions in the background, the real problem arises when one chooses a pronoun to refer to God *(Ifray).*

Christians among the Pévé tribe had been converted by evangelists from another tribe, the Moundang. The Moundang word for God was also feminine, namely, *Masing.* However, the third-person singular Moundang pronoun, *ako,* is gender neutral: it can mean either "he" or "she," the determination being supplied by the context. Pévé Christians had learned from the Moundang that God should be addressed as Father, so they had come to think of *Ifray* as merely a name for God and used the male pronoun *Mum* ("he"), rather than *Ta* ("she"), to refer to him.

But now that their language was being reduced to writing and the Scriptures were being translated into Pévé, Venberg pushed a little harder to sort things out. Why not use *Bafray,* "Father," to refer to God, instead of *Ifray?* The Pévé believers strenuously objected that this would be introducing a foreign God, an alien God. Then why not use *Ta* ("she") as the pronoun, to preserve formal agreement? The Pévé believers did not think that was necessary, since they did not really think of (Christian) *Ifray* as having a sex. *Ifray* was merely a name, and the Christians were used to referring to this God with *Mum,* the masculine pronoun.

Further exploration, however, disclosed something else. When the Christians tried to share their faith with unbelievers among the Pévé, their "solution" struck hearers as essentially alien. Even some church people used *Mum* ("he") to refer to God in church, but *Ta* ("she") to refer to God when they were on their own or in their families. Outsiders who heard Christians referring to *Ifray* as "he" and as the "Father of our Lord Jesus Christ" thought the breach of concord bizarre and asked if they would have to change their talk if they became Christians. But if the Pévé Christians switched to using feminine pronouns to speak of God, then the "she" who was "mother" of Jesus was likely to be understood as Mary, not God.

I need not here pursue how Venberg and the Pévé Christians finally handled the matter in their translation. I'm not certain that their resolution was the best one—but of course, I wasn't there! I am merely trying to show how extraordinarily difficult translation problems bound up with gender systems may be.

Nor can one write off this example as peculiarly difficult because one is dealing with a language interlocked with tribal religion: the grammatical gender is tied to an active myth that concerns a female god. Certainly this sort of link makes the problem more difficult in some cases, of course, but the challenges of Bible translation and how to refer to God in differing gender systems transcend the languages of African tribes. In French, while *Dieu* ("God") is masculine, *Trinité* ("Trinity") is feminine. Thus one refers to God with the masculine pronoun *il*, but to the Trinity with the feminine pronoun *elle*. "The holy God" is *le saint Dieu* (masculine singular article and adjective); "the holy Trinity" is *la sainte Trinité* (feminine singular article and adjective). Of course, this particular result of the French gender system does not occur in the Bible, but certainly it occurs in the history of Christian thought.

Some Biblical Examples

The word for "spirit" is feminine in Hebrew, neuter in Greek, and normally we use the masculine pronoun in English. In the complex expression "the Spirit of the Lord" or "the Spirit of God" in the Hebrew canon, the word "Spirit" is formally feminine, but it is treated as a feminine thirty-six times and as a masculine seven times (thus breaking gender concord).

So from this one example, if someone were to criticize the NRSV or the NIVI on the ground that these revisions include words that God did not originally cause to be written, that is, human words that people have substituted for the words of God, how should we respond? Does this demand that we use feminine pronouns for the Spirit of the Lord wherever the Old Testament

contrast, "representative generics" include expressions like "the man" in Psalm 1:1, even though men and women are included. Both representative generics and pure generics, he writes, "are inclusive references." But in order "to bring over into English the full sense of these expressions as nearly as possible, English translations should translate the pure generics in Hebrew and Greek as *pure* generics in English, and the representative generics in Hebrew and Greek as *representative* generics in English. That would preserve their distinctive nuances."[15] But if this chapter means anything, that is precisely what one cannot do unless the gender-systems of donor and receptor languages are identical. As we shall see, they are not. Dr. Grudem's argument is simply an appeal for formal equivalence. Try applying it to Qafar, where the distances are instantly more obvious. In exactly the same way that one cannot responsibly translate a Greek genitive absolute into English as an English genitive absolute *because the syntactical structures of the two languages are different,* so one cannot responsibly translate all Greek-specified genders into English as corresponding English genders, because the gender systems of the two languages are different. And so also one cannot responsibly translate all Greek generics, pure or otherwise, into corresponding pure and representative generics in English, *because the gender systems of the two languages are different,* and, on these points (I shall argue), increasingly diverging.

Not for a moment am I suggesting that all of the criticisms leveled against gender-neutral translations are misguided. Some of them, as will be clear in chapters 6 and 7, I heartily endorse. But the argument that attaches a particular formal equivalent in gender assignment to faithfulness to the Word of God is profoundly mistaken in principle. It understands neither translation nor gender systems. Even when the criticism is telling with respect to a particular passage, it does not follow that the undergirding assumptions about language and translation are believable.

5

A BRIEF EVALUATION OF THE CBT AND CS PRINCIPLES

The two sets of principles or translation guidelines printed in chapter 2 of this book are quite different in purpose, length, and comprehensiveness. Moreover, as I have already indicated, the Committee on Bible Translation principles are currently undergoing review. Quite apart from the principles themselves, one may sometimes endorse a principle and yet be discontent with the way that principle is applied; alternatively, one might be a trifle disconcerted by the sloppiness of a principle but regain confidence from the way it is applied. In any case one should start by evaluating the guidelines, so in this chapter, building on what we have gleaned about translation and about gender systems from the previous two chapters, I shall comment on the two sets of principles. Then in the next two chapters, I shall comment briefly on a substantial number of passages from the Old Testament (chapter 6) and from the New (chapter 7). Separate chapters are desirable because the donor languages for the two Testaments are different and cast up rather different problems for the translator. In chapter 8 I will look at a few passages under dispute that have considerable theological weight.

You will find it simplest to keep your finger in chapter 2 to follow the discussion in this chapter.

Reflections on the CBT Principles

CBT Principle I.C

Principle I.C could be understood in a good sense or a bad sense. Its potential for being understood in a bad sense was apparently what prompted the CBT to include the explanatory note.[1] To think of rendering what may "offend modern sensibilities" in some fashion that will remove the offense could easily open up a sinkhole into which almost any change could be dropped. Does the notion of substitutionary atonement offend modern sensibilities? Change the wording. Does what the Bible says about men and women offend modern sensibilities? Modify the text.

Yet the "note" gives examples of what CBT members had in mind, and scarcely anyone would take exception to their examples. I have not seen any written criticisms of the NIV's "one male" as a rendering of the Hebrew "one who urinates against the wall" (1 Sam. 25:22). Nor have I seen anyone become upset with the NIV's "whose genitals were like those of donkeys" for Hebrew "whose flesh was like that of a donkey" (where "flesh" in Hebrew is in this instance a metaphor for penis—Ezek. 23:20). Note the change not only in noun ("flesh" [signifying "penis"] becomes "genitals") but in number, and therefore also in the number of the verb.

Thus the examples are unexceptional, even though the principle is as broad as the proverbial barn door. It would be wise to try to recast the principle in such a way that the examples in the "note" are accommodated without leaving the way open for less acceptable changes. I can think of several ways this might be done, all of them slightly messy. I shall mention one, but approach it, as it were, through the back door.

Consider Romans 16:16: "Greet one another with a holy kiss." In chapter 1 (under "Recent Developments") we briefly reflected on this text with respect to the relationships between language and larger cultural structures. Now we may ask more pointedly: Are Christians sinning against God if they do not obey this literally? Christians in France obey it literally, of course, but few citizens of England do, and only a small percentage of American Christians. Is this failure nothing other than callous disobedience? Few would say so. One of the reasons is that the New Testament offers no theology of kissing. Kissing is not a repeatedly mentioned act full of complex, symbol-laden, theological overtones. What Paul *does* offer, in this case, is a theology of how Christians should love one another, accept one another, build one another up, welcome one another—and in Paul's culture, one of the cultural signs of such warmth was a greeting with a kiss that transcended barriers of race and status and money. The famous paraphrase "Give a hearty handshake all around" may remove the text a bit too much from the historical particularity of the first century, but it is not wrongheaded: in some of our cultures, that is the cultural equivalent.

What one must ask of the examples in the CBT's "note," then, is whether the Old Testament offers a theology of males as those who urinate against a wall, or a theology of "flesh" as a metaphor for the penis. The question answers itself. Thus the principle at stake needs to focus more narrowly than it does: it should not be left open to virtually anything that offends modern sensibilities, but should speak more narrowly of forms of expression that offend modern sensibilities where those expressions are not tied to theological themes that run through the text. Of course, translators must then decide what themes *do* run through texts and be honest about the matter.

But that sort of decision goes with the job of translation: as we have seen, translation is never a mechanical function. The point is that if we preserve "one who urinates against a wall" and thereby cause a contemporary reader to gasp at the coarseness when the original readers would have detected no coarseness, we may have preserved a more formal correspondence but we have translated badly. In the name of formal correspondence we have achieved a negative result neither intended by the author nor found in the original readers. If the author *intends* to be shocking, however, as in the Ezekiel passage, then of course this must be taken into account in the translation. Even so, the NIV's "genitals" is a responsible rendering, for the passage in Ezekiel is shocking not because of the *word* chosen but because of the nature of the comparison in the extended metaphor that likens spiritual apostasy to unbridled fornication. In English, "penis" is perhaps a more shocking *word,* but it is not the Hebrew word that is shocking. Here the CBT made a good choice.

As Professor John Stek points out in a private communication to me (February 27, 1998), even this relatively minor question of the translation of a Hebrew euphemism can have unexpected difficulties attached to it. The expression "he who urinates against a wall" occurs six times in Old Testament narrative texts—twice in 1 Samuel 25 and four times in 1 and 2 Kings. But the passage in 1 Samuel 25 carries unexpected freight not easily translated. Nabal is introduced as a "Calebite." At one level this ties him to a famous ancestor. The problem is that *caleb* in Hebrew also means "dog" (note the use of "dog" in 1 Sam. 17:43; 24:14 [24:15 MT]). Just as the author plays on the name Nabal (both "fool" and "wineskin" [he is "full of wine"]; see 1 Sam. 25:18, 25, 36), so also does the author point out that Nabal is a "Calebite," a mere dog that urinates against a wall. All of this is obvious enough in Hebrew, but puns are notoriously difficult to translate. If one includes an explanatory note for this pun, must one do so for all puns? In any case, the Hebrew euphemism "he who urinates against a wall" is suddenly a euphemism with more than a little complexity for the translator to worry over.

CBT Principle I.D

In the same way, principle I.D could be understood in a good sense or a bad sense. What some people mean by "patriarchalism," others take to be God's beneficent ordering of society. The latter would certainly want to reject "patriarchalism" that is nothing more than boorish exploitation of women, but they have learned to be wary of some in the egalitarian camp who use the emotionally laden term to besmirch any view that does not tally with their own egalitarianism. Principle I.D is so imprecisely expressed it could be used to rewrite substantial chunks of the Bible, changing themes that are there, no matter how uncomfortable they make some people feel.

On the other hand, principle I.D could be read in a far more conservative way. It could be using "patriarchalism" to refer to forms of linguistic expression, including grammatical gender, that are seriously at odds with the gender system in contemporary English. In such cases, preserving formal equivalence may actually be bad translation. We have already seen, for instance, that "sons of Israel" in Hebrew may be used to refer to groups of both men and women Israelites. To preserve the formal equivalent in a translation into English would be misleading and carry a negative overtone, and on both these counts be a bad translation. People of goodwill may disagree about the extent to which English words such as "man" and "he" may still function generically today—I shall say more about that debate later—but all sides will agree, I think, that "sons" and "brothers," in both Hebrew and Greek Scripture, not infrequently include people of both sexes. There is therefore nothing intrinsically wrong or evil about sacrificing the formal equivalent for something that better captures the meaning of the Hebrew text. It may be that by principle I.D, the CBT had in view only these kinds of problems. One hopes that is the case, for it seems to be implied by the closing sentence: "care must be taken not to distort the intent of the original texts." Still, the principle is not very carefully worded.[2]

CBT Principles I.E, I.F, and I.G

Principles I.E, I.F, and I.G would, I suspect, be happily embraced by the CBMW as well as by the CBT. Taken together, however, they prompt some interesting reflections. One should at least ask why the masculine gender of "God" is preserved, while the feminine or neuter gender of the words for "Spirit," including most of the pronouns that preserve grammatical agreement, are rendered in English as masculines. There is, I think, good reason. In the case of the other two persons of the Godhead, we are not dealing merely with the grammatical gender of words like "God," but with ascriptions such as "Father" and "Son" which, both in Hebrew and Greek, align grammatical gender with sexual gender, which alignment is again preserved in the pronominal gender system of English. Nor is this a merely "accidental" phenomenon bound up with the peculiar languages in which the biblical revelation was given. Although God is certainly not a sexual being in the same sense in which human beings are sexual beings, he has chosen to disclose himself in Scripture as the One who is addressed as Father,[3] who is the Father of our Lord and Savior Jesus Christ (and this latter relationship, between "the Father" and "the Son," is worked out in such complex detail [for example, John 5:16–30] that it cannot be touched without massive rewriting of substantive content). Further, since the mother of Jesus is Mary, even on pragmatic grounds it is impractical to lose the distinctive "Father" for God himself.

CBT Principle II(5)

The reasoning behind principle II(5) escapes me. The CBT's commitment to preserve the maleness of a human referent in cultural contexts where only males would occupy the post is commendable. So why is an English equivalent that loses that historical specificity preferable? I would argue that in at least one of the pairs the CBT here offers by way of example, namely, "bowman"/"archer," the latter term is preferable simply because the former sounds slightly obsolete. If "archer" loses the specificity of the sexual gender in "bowman," so be it. But the logic of the CBT's position, as stated, is a little hard to fathom. One might, I suppose, argue that "archer," "worker," and "rower" focus on the essential activity of the referent, and it is unnecessary to send up flags as to what gender the person is, since even though such persons were invariably male in the ancient world that fact makes little difference to the point of this or that passage. That, at least, would be an argument worth evaluating; perhaps that is what CBT had in mind. My only hesitation—and it is a balance of judgments—is that I am loath to lose historical particularity.

CBT Principle II(6)

Principle II(6) needs some expansion or clarification. If there is repeated male reference in the donor text, and such reference is to people who were, historically speaking, males, it is difficult to see why the references should be thinned out. On the other hand, if repeated male reference has primarily to do with the nature of the grammatical gender system in the language and has little to do with the sexual gender of the human referents, the principle makes good sense and is entirely responsible (granted, of course, that the English language is changing as the CBT people think it is).

CBT Principle II(8)

Principle II(8) is heavily criticized by the CSG and related documents. In my view, one must tackle this matter case by case. As we shall see, the critics seem to assume that it is always inappropriate to render a singular by a plural. Even from what has been surveyed in the previous two chapters, I do not see how that position can be consistently maintained. Deuteronomy 12, for instance, and several other Old Testament chapters abound in singular/plural switches whose significance is highly disputed among most commentators, and the wisest of them throw up their hands and say they are uncertain what function these switches have. One is dealing with *systems* of language structures; one does not have the right to assume that singular and plural forms function in Hebrew and Greek exactly as they function in English. But even in English, we sometimes use the singular generically. This choice may be occasioned by an author's "feel" for something nebulous called "style" in a particular context.

But *even if* (and it is a big "if") the purpose of a singular form is to say something about the individual, if the only corresponding individual expression in English is one which is gender-specific and will be read in those parts of the English-speaking world where such gender specificity carries overtones of bigotry *not carried by the donor text,* then the responsible translator is faced with an awkward choice: Preserve the singular form and project bigotry, or go with a plural form and lose the individual reference. We have seen how the translation enterprise is riddled with choices of this sort: translation is treason. One may, of course, legitimately disagree with a translator's choice in some of these catch-22 dilemmas. But one may not responsibly disagree with a translator's choice in such matters in a way that intimates that the other side is perverse, incompetent, or disrespectful of Scripture. To argue that the donor text is singular and therefore that using anything other than the singular in the receptor text is necessarily flawed is a bad argument. That presupposes that the gender systems, number systems, overtones of words, and the like are exactly the same in the two languages.

Consider an example that has been repeatedly discussed in the literature. In the NIV, Psalm 1:1–2 reads, "Blessed is the man who does not walk in the counsel of the wicked. . . . But his delight is in the law of the LORD." The NIVI renders the same passage, "Blessed are those who do not walk in the counsel of the wicked. . . . But their delight is in the law of the Lord." The Hebrew, of course, is singular. The critics say that this is a betrayal of the Hebrew singular, which has been sacrificed on the altar of a feminist agenda. Moreover, is there not a special reason to preserve the singular here, namely, that the psalmist switches to the plural in 1:4–6, and the distinction should be maintained?

Defenders of the NIVI respond in several ways. Although doubtless there are some of feminist persuasion who are offended by "man" in the NIV, not a few of the CBT translators are complementarians. Their opinion on language use in growing segments of English-speaking America and Britain, however, is that "man" is increasingly understood, for whatever reason, to refer to the male of the human species, and *that is not what the psalmist was saying.* So for the sake of accuracy in translation, it is better *not* to use "man" and the corresponding pronouns "his" and "he" in subsequent verses. What, then, are the options? One might try, "Blessed is the person who . . ."—but although that might satisfy 1:1a, the masculine pronouns are not thereby relieved in verses 2–3 since English's pronominal gender system marks the singular pronoun for gender. Better therefore to go with the plural, since the plural pronoun in English is not marked for gender. Besides, these defenders might say, when plural statements of this sort are made, English readers apply them individually anyway. For instance, Jesus says, "Blessed are those who are persecuted because of righteousness" (Matt. 5:10)—and each individual believer asks himself or herself (those awkward pronouns again!) exactly how this beatitude applies to him or her (them?). So the formal loss of the individual referent, in the view of the defenders of the NIVI, is not a serious one. Moreover, the plurals in 1:4–6, they say, may not be offered as a contrast to the singular forms in 1:1–3, but as an alternative stylistic form. All sides recognize that the singular form can be a collective; why not here?

Now if at this juncture the critics reply that in their view the balance of judgments favors the conclusion that the loss is worse by opting for the plural form, and advance some reasons for this judgment, and the defenders of the NIVI go the other way, and give some reasons for their judgment, and the two sides agree to disagree, that disagreement may be painful and difficult, but neither side is thereby questioning the motives or competence of the other side. But if one side insists that the other, by its translation judgment in this instance, is twisting the very words of God or the like,[4] it should be obvious by now that it is betraying ignorance of translation problems and the nature of gender and number systems in different languages. That side is merely blessing its own translation preferences with divine sanction.

Consider another example.[5] Here is a section of Psalm 34, quoted from the KJV but with the singulars and plurals marked:

> [15]The eyes of the Lord are upon the righteous [plural], and his ears are open unto their [plural] cry.
>
> [16]The face of the Lord is against them [plural] that do evil, to cut off the remembrance of them [plural] from the earth.
>
> [17]The righteous cry [plural], and the Lord heareth, and delivereth them [plural] out of all their [plural] troubles.
>
> [18]The Lord is nigh unto them [plural] that are of a broken heart [singular]; and saveth such [plural] as be of a contrite spirit [singular].
>
> [19]Many are the afflictions of the righteous [singular; LXX has plural]: but the Lord delivereth him [singular; LXX has "them," plural] out of them all.
>
> [20]He keepeth all his [singular; LXX has "their," plural] bones: not one of them is broken.
>
> [21]Evil shall slay the wicked [singular; LXX has plural]: and they [plural] that hate the righteous [singular] shall be desolate.

[22]The LORD redeemeth the soul [singular; LXX has "souls," plural] of his servants [plural]: and none of them [plural] that trust in him shall be desolate.

One cannot fail to note that both the "righteous" and the "wicked" can be in either singular or plural. There may be structural reasons for this switching—the stuff of discussions in commentaries. But granted the limitations of the English gender system, it is extraordinarily difficult to think how all of these number specificities are likely to be preserved in natural English.

Consider the furor when some translations replaced "thou" with "you." This was a debate over number, not gender. The fact is that "thou" is marked for number (singular), while "you" is not. The progressives said that "you" should prevail because "thou" conveyed an old-fashioned tone that was not found in the donor text; the conservatives argued that both Hebrew and Greek second-person pronouns distinguish between singular and plural pronouns, and we would be losing something important of the Word of God if we lost that distinction. Some conservatives also argued that the archaic form should at least be preserved in direct address to God (in prayer, for example), because it was more respectful. Progressives replied that the donor texts did not convey respect by choosing archaizing forms. On these matters some Bible translations went one way, some the other. The overwhelming majority have now lined up with "you,"[6] simply because the continued changes in spoken English made that choice all but inevitable. That is the challenge of translation. It does not add to the clarity of the debate to charge either side with Scripture twisting.

CBT Principles II(13) and II(19)

Principle II(13) is nicely put, but as we shall see in the next chapter, not always well executed. I suspect that in the light of the current debate, appeal to principle II(19) might be made much more often in the future: explanatory notes may help to assuage the worst fears.

CBT Principle II(20)

Whatever one thinks of the final principle, II(20), it illustrates perfectly some of the tensions that translators face. On the one hand, the CBT members rightly wish to preserve the historical particularity of the biblical cultures and therefore opt to preserve male-specific references in biblical texts where only males would occupy those cultural slots at the time.

But the three exceptions are intriguing. The first *(a)* makes an exception of passages that are universally applicable. I think this is unobjectionable if by "universally applicable" is meant something like "the utterance is universally applicable, *including application even at the time the utterance was first given,* even though the formal categories are male." The two examples provided are helpful: "No servant can serve two masters. Either *he* will hate. . . . You cannot serve both God and Money" (Luke 16:13 NIV; compare 17:31–33). The servant in this utterance is male; nevertheless, the application concerns followers of Jesus of both sexes in every time and place, including the first century. Either one must introduce a footnote explaining this, or one opts for something like the NIVI: "No one can be a slave to two masters. Either *you* will hate. . . . You cannot be a slave to both God and Money." Note the changes. Gender-inclusive language in the first line does not handle the pronoun in the second. In this case the solution has been to draw back the second-person pronoun from the last line into the second line. I do not find that objectionable in this case. The NIVI has changed "servant" to "slave": here the NIVI is right, and the NIV is wrong.

The second exception *(b)* does not, in my view, make a case. If the extended passage loses its gender specificity (as in Luke 14:31–35), why not lose it in English at about the same place? I see little advantage in losing it earlier, given the CBT's commitment to maintaining historical specificity.

The third exception *(c)* appeals to universal modern circumstances, and gives Matthew 10:24 as an example: "A student is not above his teacher, nor a servant above his master" (NIV); compare "Students are not above their teachers, nor servants above their masters" (NIVI). I am happy with the NIVI's rendering, but the principle as articulated leaves a door open big enough to drive a tank through. For further reflection on the move from singular expressions to plurals, see below.

Reflections on the CS Principles

By and large, the CSG are open to far more and far more serious linguistic objections than the CBT principles. This is not to say that they are always wrong: in application, these principles in the hands of the NIV and NRSV critics sometimes point out translation weaknesses that should be remedied. But the principles themselves do not stand up very well. Probably this is as much because of how they were generated as anything else: they were generated not over a sustained period by a group of scholars engaged in the difficult work of translation but comparatively quickly by a group of scholars whose mission was to critique the translation of others.

CS Principle A.1

Principle A.1 says that "generic use of 'he, him, his, himself' should be employed to translate *generic* 3rd person masculine singular pronouns in Hebrew, Aramaic and Greek" (emphasis mine). What this assumes is that English generic use of such pronouns exactly mirrors the generic use of the pronouns in the donor languages. In general terms, one should be suspicious of such assumptions: gender systems differ from language to language.

It would be true to say that the English of two or three decades ago used such pronouns as "he," "his," and so on in a generic sense more frequently than is common today. In that sense principle A.1 is an appeal to conservatism in language—which becomes obvious when CBMW scholars devote energy to trying to prove that the English language is not changing. I shall argue in chapter 9 that that is a bit like Canute trying to hold back the tide. Even so, if the critics of inclusive-language Bible translations were merely articulating their preference for conservatism in English form (like those who long preferred "thou" and other archaisms when most English speakers had abandoned them), that would be an acceptable position with which others might disagree. But these critics are insisting that their position is *more faithful* to Scripture. And there, they are simply mistaken.

In addition to the criticisms of this position that have already been raised, observe three factors.

First, the second part of A.1 betrays the fact that the critics are thinking at the level of English gloss rather than at the level of meaning. They write, "However, substantival participles such as *ho pisteuōn* can often be rendered in inclusive ways, such as 'the one who believes' rather than 'he who believes.'" True, *ho pisteuōn* is often rendered, in elementary Greek instruction textbooks, "the one who believes," or the like. But strictly speaking, *ho* is the *masculine* article, and the participle, as determined by the article, is masculine as well. Of course, this is a generic usage, but so also is the usage generic in many occurrences of the Hebrew or Greek masculine *pronoun*. Why the double standard, except for the influence of English gloss? The donor languages do not encourage a distinction in translation approaches based on the gender of these parts of speech, since within their own gender systems the masculine is retained.

Second, the insistence on using English masculine pronouns for masculine pronouns in the donor languages hides an ambiguity that has not yet been addressed. Compare the following three passages, each cited first from the NIV and then from the NIVI and the NRSV:[7]

John 6:44

NIV: "No one can come to me unless the Father who sent me draws *him*; and I will raise *him* up at the last day."

NIVI: "No-one can come to me unless the Father who sent me draws them, and I will raise them up at the last day."

NRSV: "No one can come to me unless drawn by the Father who sent me; and I will raise that person up on the last day."

John 6:51

NIV: "If anyone eats of this bread, *he* will live forever."

NIVI: "Whoever eats of this bread will live for ever."

NRSV: "Whoever eats of this bread will live forever."

John 6:56

NIV: "Whoever eats my flesh and drinks my blood remains in me, and I in *him*."

NIVI: "Those who eat my flesh and drink my blood remain in me, and I in them."

NRSV: "Those who eat my flesh and drink my blood abide in me, and I in them."

In the first of these three passages, the Greek text uses the pronoun *autos* in the accusative case. The CS principle A.1 demands that we retain "him" in English. Theologically, of course, "him" both in Greek and in the NIV must be understood generically: the text is certainly not saying that God draws to himself only male human beings. The NIVI, holding that "him" is less and less able to function generically, opts for the third-person plural "them," which is not marked for gender. This introduces a formal breach of concord with the singular "no-one" (though certainly some speech patterns are heading in that direction today). The NRSV solves the problem by dissolving the first "him" into a passive structure, and transmuting the second "him" into the slightly cumbersome but certainly gender-neutral "that person."

But whatever one thinks of this example, the next one introduces quite a different problem. Despite the NIV's rendering with its pronoun "he," the Greek actually has no pronoun. The subject is established by the inflection of the finite verb *zēsei* "[x] will live." The inflection is marked for number and person, *but not for gender*. So far as the mere inflection is concerned, the verbal form might be rendered "he/she/it will live." The NIV inserted "he" because English structure demands a separate pronoun. Moreover, when the NIV did so, "he" functioned generically more frequently than it does today. The NIVI and NRSV circumnavigate the problem by rendering the Greek "if" clause as a "whoever" clause, which then functions as the subject of "will live." Strictly speaking, of course, principle A.1 does not address such circumstances (which are exceedingly common in the New Testament). But they illustrate the problem of translating across languages with different morphological systems and different gender systems. Neither the NIV nor the NIVI/NRSV *can* retain formal equivalence here. The NIV preserves a clause with "if-structure," but then over-specifies gender by choosing a gender-marked personal pronoun (since English does not offer the option of having an unmarked subject specified by verbal inflection); the NIVI and NRSV preserve the lack of gender markedness by slightly modifying the subordinate clause.

The third example brings up yet another problem. Principle A.1 concedes that participial constructions such as *ho pisteuōn* may be rendered "the one who believes" or the like (even though these constructions are masculine), but even this turns out to be not much of a concession if a little farther on in the same sentence the referent of such a participle is referred to using a masculine pronoun—for then the first part of A.1 kicks in. That is what has occurred in John 5:26: "Whoever eats my flesh and drinks my blood remains in me, and I in *him*" (NIV). All sides agree that the "him" in Greek is generic, even though *formally* marked for grammatical gender. Both the NIVI and NRSV preserve that generic meaning by avoiding an English pronoun that is increasingly viewed as not only marked for grammatical gender in English, but in the usage of many is semantically tied to sexual gender. To do this, they resort to the plural. *Both* translations "lose" a little something or "gain" a little something, because the structures of donor and receptor languages are different.

Third, one suspects that principle A.1, which has not addressed the fundamental issues in which it is enmeshed, has as its primary goal the elimination of renderings that "get around" the use of such masculine pronouns as "he" and "his"—and this becomes clear in the second principle on the list, which is really the negative counterpart to the first principle. In other words, A.1 mandates that "he" and so on be used; A.2 forbids that other expressions be used.

CS Principle A.2

In part I have dealt with principle A.2 not only implicitly in the previous two chapters, but also in my discussion above of CBT principle II(8). The prohibition articulated in A.2, even with the barely conceded exception at the end, does not demonstrate an evenhanded grasp of how gender systems in different languages work and of the kinds of choices translators have to make. Implicitly, as we have seen, it argues for a conservatism in language use (which is a responsible position, whether or not one agrees with it) but interprets that position in a framework of orthodoxy that sets those who disagree with it outside the pale. But I should add a few more observations.

First, Dr. Mark L. Strauss[8] and others have pointed out that sometimes when the New Testament cites the Old, it renders a Hebrew generic singular with a Greek plural. We may select three examples from Paul's use of the Old Testament: (1) "How beautiful on the mountains are the feet of *him* who brings good news" (Isa. 52:7);[9] "As it is written, 'How beautiful are the feet of *those* who bring good news'" (Rom. 10:15). (2) "There is no fear of God before *his* eyes" (Ps. 36:1); "As it is written . . . 'There is no fear of God before *their* eyes'" (Rom. 3:10, 18). (3) "Blessed is *he* whose transgressions are forgiven, whose sins are covered" (Ps. 32:1); "David says the same thing . . . 'Blessed are *they* whose transgressions are forgiven, whose sins are covered'" (Rom. 4:6, 7).

I am certainly not suggesting that singulars may be translated into plurals indiscriminately. In due course we shall see some instances where certain kinds of generic singulars should not be rendered as plurals. But at the very least, one must conclude, from Paul's own habits, that the apostle does not think something of truth is lost when he renders a singular by a plural. In the last of the three cases (Ps. 32:1 in Rom. 4:6–7), he is quoting the LXX. The apostle neither condemns the translation nor reverts to the Hebrew to retain greater accuracy.

Second, it does not help the discussion to think of language in the wooden categories of what might be called lexical exegesis. Dr. Wayne Grudem has offered some telling criticisms of some inclusive-language renderings: we shall sample some of them in the next two chapters. Certainly it is the case that the errors in judgment are not all on one side of this debate. Moreover, I greatly applaud Dr. Grudem's desire to take the Word of God seriously. Nevertheless, on this issue his constant insistence that the singular refers to the individual and the plural refers to a collection of people is linguistically unconvincing and contrary to experience. For example, he compares James 5:14–15 in the RSV and the NRSV.[10] The former reads, "Is any among you sick? Let him call for the elders of the church, and let them pray over him . . . and the prayer of faith will save the sick man, and the Lord will raise him up." In the NRSV, this has become, "Are any among you sick? They should call for the elders of the church and have them pray over them. . . . The prayer of faith will save the sick, and the Lord will raise them up." Dr. Grudem writes, "The situation that comes to mind is entirely different; James wrote about a private home with one person sick, but now it looks like a hospital ward! The meaning has been changed. This is not accurately translating the Bible; it is rewriting the Bible."[11]

This strong charge, I said, is "linguistically unconvincing and contrary to experience." *(a)* It is linguistically unconvincing because it fails to wrestle with the way translation works. I invite him to apply the same sort of criteria as what he here presupposes when we translate the biblical texts into some of the more alien languages whose gender systems I briefly summarized in chapter 4. Sometimes *there is no choice* but to lose one way of saying something to get at the heart of the content a somewhat different way. In English there are several choices. None is perfect, because our gender system— whether our gender and number system of the Elizabethan period or of fifty years ago or of the past two decades—does not mesh exactly with the gender and number systems of Hebrew, Aramaic, and Greek. This is no more "rewriting" the Bible than any translation: translation is treason. *(b)* It is contrary to experience. I very much doubt that the rendering of the NRSV makes many readers think of hospital wards. That is because both in the Bible and in ordinary contemporary English plurals are sometimes used to command or forbid things, or to hold up examples, that are then *individually* appropriated: we have seen instances of this already. The formal plural in such cases does not lose or exclude the individual. Behind Dr. Grudem's humor is an unrealistic caricature. He would not be pleased, I suspect, if an opponent caricatured the RSV: "What is this? Did the early church have sick men and no sick women? Or was it considered righteous to pray for the Christian men who fell sick, but not for the Christian women?" He might rightly reply that the male references in the RSV were at the time (1952) understood in a generic sense. He might even reply that they should still be so understood today. But let us suppose that English moves on to the place where "he" refers *exclusively* to the male. Would he himself not then be forced to concede that using "he" in English in this passage would be transmitting positively *false* information? But some of us are convinced that the language is changing. For those segments of the population for whom such changes have already taken place (including more than a few complementarians), the NRSV is not "rewriting the Bible." Rather, it is faced with typical choices facing all translators and offers a solution that cannot responsibly be written off by caricature.

Third, although the change from third-person pronouns to second- or first-person pronouns (since the third-person singular pronouns in English are marked for gender but not the second- and first-person pronouns) is a little more difficult, again one should be cautious about blanket condemnations. Consider some examples:

Proverbs 20:24

RSV: "A man's steps are ordered by the LORD."
NRSV: "All our steps are ordered by the LORD."

Matthew 15:11

NIV: "What goes into a man's mouth does not make him 'unclean.'"
NIVI: "What goes into your mouth does not make you 'unclean.'"

Galatians 6:7

RSV: "Whatever a man sows, that he will also reap."
NRSV: "You reap whatever you sow."

James 1:20

RSV: "For the anger of man does not work the righteousness of God."
NRSV: "For your anger does not produce God's righteousness."

James 2:14

RSV: "What does it profit . . . if a man says he has faith but has not works?"

NRSV: "What good is it . . . if you say you have faith, but do not have works?"

Dr. Grudem has objected that, in the fourth instance above (James 1:20), "readers might well think that James is speaking only about the anger of Christians. . . . But in fact James is making a more general statement about the anger of human beings. James did not say 'your anger'; he said 'the anger of man.'"[12] Similarly, with respect to Galatians 6:7: "Readers will probably think that Paul is speaking only of something that is true of Christians. . . . But in fact Paul is making a much more general statement about human conduct, and about people generally."[13]

I agree that switching persons is at least potentially misleading. Nevertheless, it does not follow that such a switch is invariably wrong or perverse or a rewriting of Scripture. Three things must be said. *(a)* Once again, the argument is an attack, not an evaluation. If the English language is changing in the way the translators of the NRSV and NIVI believe it is, they cannot responsibly leave all those gender-specific words in the English text precisely because to do so would be bad translation. They would be conveying concepts and images *not* found in the donor texts. Granted, then, the limitations of English (in particular, that its pronominal gender system has no gender-neutral third-person singular pronoun), translators have only so many choices, and each of them gains and/or loses something. I am sorry to have to keep repeating the point, but it must be got across: that is the nature of translation. We should be grateful that English has as many structural parallels with, say, Greek, as it does. Pity the translator turning Greek or Hebrew into one of the North Australian languages. *(b)* "You" in English, though formally second person (and not marked for number), in some usages functions very much like *on* in French or *man* in German. If someone says "You only die once" or "Life is hard and then you die" or "You get what you pay for"[14] or "You should brush your teeth after every meal," the "you" in each sentence will not be understood to refer in some exclusive sense only to the person or persons addressed. Some first-person plural idioms have the same sort of flexibility: "We have to die some time," and so on. The clause does not suggest that others may not have to die some time. "You" is most likely to function in this way in English in aphoristic utterances—very much like Galatians 6:7. *(c)* Biblical writers themselves sometimes use a similar approach, sometimes in conversation with "theoretical" opponents. Ironically, one of those places is in James 2, where Dr. Grudem, as we have seen, finds difficulty with the NRSV rendering of 2:14. A bare five verses later, James continues: "You believe that God is one; you do well. . . . Do you want to be shown, you shallow man, that faith apart from works is barren?" (James 2:19–20 RSV). Certainly James himself is not restricting the "you" to Christians. In other words, I fear that there is a lexical woodenness to Dr. Grudem's interpretations that vitiates some of his criticisms of gender-neutral translations.

CS Principles A.3, A.4, and A.5

We may evaluate together principles A.3, A.4, and A.5 because all three have to do with the word "man" and the corresponding terms in Hebrew and Greek. In sum, the CSG stipulate that *(a)* "man" should ordinarily be used to designate the human race, *(b)* Hebrew *ʾîsh* should ordinarily be rendered "man" (or "men" in the plural), *(c)* Greek *anēr* should almost always be so rendered, *(d)* singular *anthrōpos* should be rendered "man" when it refers to a male human being, and *(e)* plural *anthrōpoi* may be translated "people" when it refers to people in general.

To begin with, three linguistic principles are being overlooked. *(a)* The most important is the one we have observed again and again—the assumption that the donor word occupies the same semantic range as the receptor word, when the evidence often flies in the face of the assumption. *(b)* At one point there is an important confusion between meaning and referent. *(c)* Implicitly there is also a confusion between meaning and translation gloss—but this latter point I shall pick up again in chapter 8. Here it will be enough to fasten on the first two linguistic problems. It will be simplest to begin by reflecting on the donor words.

First, the two most common Hebrew words often rendered "man" or "men" are *ʾādām* and *ʾîsh* (and there are others: see below). The CSG do not specifically mention the former, though it is treated in CBMW literature. But it is worth reflecting on *ʾādām*. Its most important theological connections are bound up with passages in the opening chapters of Genesis: I shall treat them in chapter 8. Nevertheless the lexica point out that *ʾādām* can have a range of meanings, including "humanity," "a human being," and "a male human being." When God says, "I will blot out man [*ʾādām*] whom I have created" (Gen. 6:7 RSV), he is not referring to an individual male human, nor to all male humans, but to the human race save Noah and his family. Hence the NIV's "mankind," and the NIVI's "human race." By contrast, in the clause "Whoever sheds the blood of man [*ʾādām*]" (Gen. 9:6 RSV), the word is not referring to the human race, nor to male human beings only, nor to a specific human being (male or female), but to any human being. The NIV has "man"; the NIVI has "human being." Granted the sensitivities that read "man" in an exclusive sense, it is difficult not to conclude that the NIVI is an improvement. Does one want to give the impression that the imposition of capital punishment for murder is applicable only to the murder of males?

Second, although the Hebrew word *ʾîsh* has a narrower semantic range than *ʾādām,* and may often rightly be rendered "man," there are many exceptions, some of them distinctly idiomatic. Consider the eighty or so times it occurs in conjunction with *rēʿa* (often rendered "neighbor"). The KJV rendering of Exodus 11:2 is: "Speak now in the ears of the people, and let every *man* borrow of *his neighbour,* and every *woman* of *her neighbour,* jewels of silver, and jewels of gold." Here is the pairing of these two Hebrew words. Seven chapters later, the KJV renders the same pairing, "When they have a matter, they come unto me; and I judge between *one* and *another,* and I do make them know the statutes of God, and his laws" (Exod. 18:16)—which, incidentally, is often how the LXX renders it, thus losing the formal gender markedness of the Hebrew. It is difficult to see how this is misguided. The word *ʾîsh* on its own is rendered "person" by the NKJV in Deuteronomy 24:16 ("a person shall be put to death for his own sin"). Each person (*ʾîsh*) is to gather as much manna as needed (Exod. 16:16): it is far from clear that only the men were to do the gathering. Similarly, the Lord rewards "each person [*ʾîsh*] according to what he has done" (Ps. 62:12 [62:13 MT]).[15] Are only the men afflicted with tumors in 1 Samuel 5:9, or the "people" of the city, young and old? There are many such examples where a translator must decide.

Third, although the parallelisms of Hebrew poetry are no sure guide to the way terms work in nonpoetical Hebrew, they can be very instructive. In the Book of Job, for instance, four different nouns are used that are commonly rendered into English by "man" or "men." They are: *ʾādām* (twenty-seven times), *ʾîsh* (and its plural, *ʾănāshîm*) (forty-two times), *ʾĕnôsh* (eighteen times), and *geber* (fifteen times). The following are easily verified in a Hebrew lexicon; they were first drawn to my attention in an unpublished paper by Professor John Stek:[16]

4:17	Can *ʾĕnôsh* be more righteous than God? Can *geber* be more pure than his Maker?
10:4, 5	Do you have eyes of flesh *(bāśār)?* Do you see as *ʾĕnôsh* sees? Are your days like those of *ʾĕnôsh* or your years like those of *geber?*

14:10   But *geber* dies and is laid low;
               ʾādām breathes his last and is no more.

16:21   on behalf of *geber* he pleads with God
               as *ben-ʾādām* pleads for his friend.

25:4, 6   How then can *ʾĕnôsh* be righteous before God?
               How can one born of woman be pure?

               how much less *ʾĕnôsh*, who is but a maggot—
               ben-ʾādām, who is only a worm.

32:21   I will show partiality to no *ʾîsh,*
               nor will I flatter *ʾādām.*

33:15–17   In a dream, in a vision of the night
               when deep sleep falls on *ʾănāshîm*
               as they slumber in their beds,
               he may speak in the ears of *ʾănāshîm*
               and terrify them with warnings,
               to turn *ʾādām* from wrongdoing
               and keep *geber* from pride.

34:11   He repays *ʾādām* for what he has done;
               he brings upon *ʾîsh* what his conduct deserves.

34:34   *ʾănāshîm* of understanding declare,
               wise *geber* who hear me say to me. . . .

35:8   Your wickedness affects only *ʾîsh* like yourself,
               and your righteousness only *ben-ʾādām.*

36:25   *Kol-ʾādām* has/have seen it;
               ʾĕnôsh gazes/gaze on it from afar.

37:7   So that *kol-ʾādām* he has made may know his
                  work,
               he stops *kol-ʾanshê* [or *kol-ʾănāshîm?*] from
                  his/their labor.

38:26   to water a land where no *ʾîsh* lives,
               a desert with no *ʾādām* in it.

It does not seem possible to discover a fixed pattern to the parallelism. It follows that sharp distinctions in meaning between any two of these terms of the sort that says they cannot occupy the same semantic space, given the right context, is wrong. Moreover, with the possible exception of Job 34:34, there is no reason to think that the referents are all male, even though the grammatical gender is male. In other words, the reference is to human beings. As for singulars and plurals, note that the singular expressions *ʾĕnôsh* and *geber* in 4:17 are followed in 4:19–21 with plurals, which entails the conclusion that the singular nouns in 4:17 must be taken as collectives. In several instances, the rhetorical sharpness of the singular form is not greatly lost by pluralizing it, if there are good reasons intrinsic to the receptor language for doing so (for example, 10:4–5). Note that some passages mingle plural and singular forms (33:15–17), or use a modifier such as *kol-* ("all, every") to signal the intent. Further, the three instances of *ben-ʾādām* ("son of man") carry no special messianic overtones, and in these contexts are semantically equivalent to *ʾîsh* or *geber* or *ʾĕnôsh*. It follows that English cannot be expected to mirror Hebrew singulars and plurals by its own singulars and plurals, and that principle A.4 is too mechanically restrictive.[17] There are many more such examples in the poetic literature.

Fourth, the Greek word *anēr* is more restrictive. It normally refers to the male human being, sometimes to the husband. But there are a few passages that give us pause. James 1:20 denounces "the anger of man [*anēr*]," which "does not work the righteousness of God" (RSV). Is this dismissing only male anger, or "human anger" (NIVI)? In Acts 17:34, we are told that "[a] few men [plural of *anēr*] became followers of Paul and believed" (NIV)—among whom was at least one woman. Did only the "men" of Gennesaret bring their sick to Jesus (Matt. 14:35 RSV, NIV)? Or was it the "people" (NRSV, NIVI)? It is hard to be sure. Certainly one needs to be careful. But it is worth noting that the standard lexicon for the Greek of the New Testament and early Christian literature[18] lists as one of the lexical meanings that the word can serve as the equivalent of *tis,* "someone." (On *tis,* see further below.) In the plural, the expression then simply means "people." Moreover, an idiomatic expression such as "man for man" means something like "individually" without for a moment being restricted to individual males. Further, because (as the lexicon also points out) *anēr* in some contexts means a "man" in contrast to a "boy," it can slip over into the notion of ethical maturity, ethical perfection. Is it maleness that is fundamentally at issue in James 3:2, which the lexicon here cites? The NIV reads: "If anyone is never at fault in what he says, he is a perfect man, able to keep his whole body in check." Does James intend to imply that this valuation is not true when applied to women? In other words, by extension *anēr* has come to mean what we would call a "mature person" or the like. Hence the NIVI: "Those who are never at fault in what they say are perfect, able to keep their whole body in check."[19]

Still, when all is said and done, I agree that *anēr* most commonly means a "man," that is, a male human being. Unlike *anthrōpos,* that is the "default" position, apart from compelling contextual evidence. Of course, that occasionally leaves the translator with some difficult exegetical judgments. When Peter addresses the crowd on the day of Pentecost as "Men [plural of *anēr*] of Israel" (Acts 2:14), is he excluding women? Well, he may be: if this takes place in the Temple court where men are allowed and not women, it would explain this use of terminology. But that is far from certain. On the assumption that Peter was not speaking in that court, and that *anēr* here carries an exceptional sense, the NIVI offers "People of Israel." It is a judgment call based on a balance of probabilities. But precisely because the "default" meaning of *anēr* is "male human being" or "husband," even if sometimes there is a stretch toward "human being," there are some places where the NIVI has probably been too loose (see examples in chapter 7).

Fifth, the CSG make a distinction between the singular and plural forms of *anthrōpos.* I doubt if this can be sustained. One must not overlook the frequency with which the Greek singular *anthrōpos* actually *refers* generically to a human being. "How much more valuable is a man [*anthrōpos*] than a sheep!" (Matt. 12:12 NIV; NIVI "human being"). Is the point of the passage to assert that male human beings are more valuable than sheep, whatever else may be said for female human beings? Similarly, the NIVI has changed the NIV's "For we maintain that a *man* is justified by faith" to "For we maintain that a *person* is justified by faith" (Rom. 3:28). This is surely right.

Sixth, more important, it is far from clear to me that *anthrōpos* regularly carries the meaning "male human being" as the "default" meaning. It often *refers* to male human beings, but as always one must not rush to confuse meaning and referent. My car is a Ford. When I speak of my car, my family knows I am referring to what is in fact a Ford. But the word "car" does not *mean* "Ford." Consider, then, James 5:17 (NIV): "Elijah was a man [*anthrōpos*] just like us." The NIVI translates the same words, "Elijah was human just as we are." Doubtless Elijah was a male human being. But is it his maleness or his humanity that is at issue in the word *anthrōpos*? The *meaning* is simply "human being"; the referent, in this case, is a male of the species. Arguably, the NIVI is more, rather than less, accurate. Does James think that all his readers are exclusively males when he makes the comparison "*just as we are*"? Does he really intend to say, "Elijah was a male human being just as we are"?

The same reasoning is critical in some important christological passages. In John 10:33 NIV, some Jews accuse Jesus of blasphemy, "because you, a mere man [*anthrōpos*], claim to be God." The NIVI translates the critical expression "a mere human being." Dr. Andreas Köstenberger says that this downplays Jesus' maleness during his earthly incarnate state.[20] Dr. Köstenberger is a capable scholar and a former student whom I esteem highly.[21] But here he has made a linguistic gaffe:[22] he confuses meaning and referent. The meaning of *anthrōpos* is human being, not male human being. The Jews are accusing

Jesus of elevating not his maleness to the level of deity, but his humanness. No one is doubting Jesus' maleness; the NIVI uses only male pronouns for him. But one must not confuse meaning and referent.

Similarly, Dr. Köstenberger has raised questions about the NIVI rendering of 1 Timothy 2:5. The NIV reads: "For there is one God and one mediator between God and men [*anthrōpoi*], the man [*anthrōpos*] Christ Jesus." The NIVI renders it: "For there is one God and one mediator between God and human beings, Christ Jesus, himself human." Dr. Köstenberger says the NIVI "dilutes the maleness of Jesus during his incarnate state."[23] Others have picked up on the same charge. But is that quite fair? No one, not least the NIVI text, questions Jesus' maleness: note, for instance, the masculine pronoun "himself." There is no attempt to make him androgynous. The Greek words, singular and plural, link our humanness to Jesus' humanness. Surely no one is arguing that 1 Timothy 2:5 makes Jesus out to be a mediator between God and male human beings.[24] Again, then, the problem is a confusion over the elementary linguistic distinction between meaning and referent.[25]

Seventh, an important change made by the CBMW scholars since the first draft should probably be noted. Originally principle A.3 read that the word "man" "should ordinarily be used to designate the human race or human beings in general." The phrase "or human beings in general" was subsequently dropped.[26] We have seen too many examples that tell against including it. Moreover, the original draft made principle A.3 clash somewhat with principle A.5, which allows *anthrōpoi* to be rendered by "people" instead of "men" when it refers to "people in general"—the same phrase. By dropping the phrase and writing A.3 in its present form, of course, hundreds of examples have been deemed appropriate for inclusive language that had earlier been excluded, since the number of instances where it is the human race as such that is in view, as opposed to "human beings in general," is rather small.[27] As for the proof texts that the CS principles adduce here to support A.3 in its final form (namely, Gen. 1:26–27; 5:2; Ezek. 29:11; John 2:25), I shall comment on the Genesis passages in chapter 8 and on John 2:25 below. The only other text in this list, Ezekiel 29:11, is part of an oracle against Egypt: "No foot of man shall pass through it, and no foot of beast shall pass through it" (RSV). But surely this does not mean "no foot of humanity [considered as a race]" or the like; it simply means "no human foot" (NRSV).[28]

CS Principle A.6

Principle A.6 is valid, so far as it goes. Grammatically, the indefinite Greek pronoun *tis* is masculine or feminine; in some two-termination substantives, Greek distinguishes only neuter from masculine/feminine. Nevertheless, the real problem is that this word is often used in a sentence where a pronoun is also required—and that drives us toward the usual difficult choices.

Dr. Strauss points up another anomaly. He observes that words like *tis* are often

> really no different than the sense of masculine generic terms like *anthrōpos* and *ʾādām*. In the phrase "if someone *(anthrōpos)* is caught in a sin" (Gal. 6:1 NIV), *anthrōpos* carries precisely the same semantic content as *tis* in the phrase, "If anyone *(tis)* would come after me . . ." (Matt. 16:24 NIV). To claim that *anthrōpos* must be translated "man," but *tis* may be translated "anyone" or "someone" is another classic confusion of *form* and *meaning*. When *anthrōpos* means "anyone" why not translate it that way?[29]

CS Principle A.7

The same sort of things can be said about principle A.7, although there is a complicating factor. This pronoun does have a feminine form, namely, *oudemia*. One suspects, again, that translation gloss has prevailed over meaning (as with *ho pisteuōn,* above, in my discussion of CS principle A.1). In other words, principle A.7 is valid, but at least in part for the wrong reason. Moreover, once again the problem of the English gender-marked third-person singular pronoun returns. Consider John 6:44: "No one [*oudeis*] can come to me unless the Father who sent me draws him [*auton*]" (NIV). If we grant gender inclusiveness to "no one," even though the Greek word is grammatically masculine, and forbid it to the pronoun that refers to it and must be grammatically masculine to preserve agreement, what is the advantage? What the left hand giveth, the right hand taketh away. Once again, one can make a powerful case for either the NIVI or the NRSV renderings of this verse (cited earlier in this chapter).

CS Principle A.8

Principle A.8 is very much like A.7, with yet another wrinkle: *pas* has a feminine form in the singular *(pasa),* while in the plural it is a two-termination word (masculine and feminine have the same form). I need not repeat the implications.

Some of these matters come together in an interesting passage at the end of John 2 and the beginning of John 3. In the NIV: "Jesus would not entrust himself to them, for he knew all men [*pantas*]. He did not need man's [*tis*] testimony about man [*tou anthrōpou*], for he knew what was in a man [*tō anthrōpō*]. Now there was a man [*anthrōpos*] of the Pharisees named Nicodemus" (2:24–3:1). Contrast the NIVI: "Jesus would not entrust himself to them, for he knew all people. He did not need human testimony about them, for he knew what was in people. Now there was a Pharisee named Nicodemus." Arguably the NIVI is more accurate than the NIV in rendering *pantas* by "all people" rather than by "all men." The CSG allow the *tis* to be gender inclusive: "human testimony" is better than "man's testimony." Up to this point, the NIV has used "man" twice when even on the most formal reading of the text the word is not found in the original. The two instances of *anthrōpos* are probably not referring to the human race corporately, but to all human beings, here referred to by the use of the generic singular. The sticky point is the use of *anthrōpos* in 3:1. This makes a connection between the Nicodemus narrative and the generalizing statement in 2:24–25. One could use "man," since that is the referent, though strictly speaking the Greek word refers to Nicodemus as a human being. But if we use "man" in 3:1 while using "human beings" or "people" in 2:24–25, the *word* connection is lost, even though the *meaning* connection is retained. Once again, translators have to make choices, because the English words simply do not link up the way the Greek words do. It is partly a question of their slightly different semantic ranges, partly a question of their respective idiomatic usages. Would we ever introduce someone with an expression such as "there was a man of the Democrats" or "there was a human being of the Republicans"? So the NIVI opts for idiomatic smoothness and loses the word connection. Choices, choices: translation is treason.

CS Principles A.9 and A.10

Principle A.9, on "son of man," I shall evaluate in chapter 8. Principle A.10 is certainly valid—though as I indicated above in discussing the CBT principles, the reasons for driving toward this conclusion are more complex than first meets the eye.

CS Principle B.1

Principle B.1 is much improved in the revised guidelines. Originally neither the singular *adelphos* ("brother") nor the plural *adelphoi* ("brothers") was to be rendered "brother or sister" or "brothers and sisters" or the like. But there is plenty of unambiguous evidence, both in the New Testament and outside it, that "brothers" very often *meant* what we mean by "brothers and sisters." Thus within the New Testament, Paul can address the Philippian believers as "my brothers" (Phil.

4:1 NIV) and immediately start addressing two of the women in the church (Phil. 4:2–3; see also 1 Cor. 7:15; James 2:15). Small wonder the NIVI renders the expression "my brothers and sisters." This is not flawed translation: rather, the expanded English expression is including people who would have felt included in the Greek *adelphos* but who by and large do not feel so included in English "brothers." One may argue about the extent to which the English word "man" may still be used generically, but very little can be said in favor of still using "brothers" generically. Principle B.1 implicitly recognizes these points, in its latest draft (though not in its first), for the plural form of the word.

Why it insists on excluding inclusive language for the singular form quite escapes me. One must proceed case by case, of course. In Matthew 5:22 NIV Jesus says, "But I tell you that anyone who is angry with his brother [*adelphos*] will be subject to judgment." Is Jesus restricting the sanction to anger toward a brother, but not toward a sister? The NIVI's "brother or sister" is surely preferable. Why concede the point for the plural and deny it for the singular? This does not mean that *every* instance of *adelphos*, whether singular or plural, makes an inclusive reference. But it is difficult to credit the principle that denies the possibility of such reference to singular forms after conceding the possibility of such reference to plural forms.

CS Principle B.2

Earlier we saw that Hebrew *bānîm* ("sons"), though formally masculine, frequently includes both sons and daughters. This point principle B.2 recognizes. But it forbids translators to render the singular Hebrew *bēn* as anything other than "son," and it insists that Greek *huios/huioi* ("son"/"sons") can never mean "child"/"children" or include "sons and daughters."

Dr. Grudem provides a rationale for this position.[30] He argues that the New Testament authors "were able to speak of 'children' *(tekna)* when they wanted to (as in John 1:12, 'He gave them power to become *children* of God,' and Rom. 8:16–17, 'bearing witness with our spirit that we are *children* of God.'). But in other verses the Bible spoke of us as 'sons,' and faithful translations should not change this to 'sons and daughters' or 'children' as the NIVI did in Galatians 4:7." In the latter passage, the rendering "children," he writes, "obscures the fact that we all (men *and* women) gain standing as 'sons' and therefore the inheritance rights that belong to sons in the Biblical world."[31]

But this is methodologically mistaken. Just because some passages in the New Testament *can* distinguish between *huios* and *teknon* does not necessarily mean that the two words cannot share identical semantic ranges in pragmatic circumstances—for otherwise we have returned again to "illegitimate totality transfer." In other words, one must inspect usage in passage after passage to see if *huios* always means "son" as distinct from "child," impelled, perhaps, by overtones of what it means to be an heir.

As soon as we do this, the position collapses. In Mark 12:19, Jesus is questioned about levirate marriage, which came into play when a man died leaving no *teknon* ("child," and here surely an heir) to carry on his name. Zechariah and Elizabeth long for a *teknon* to carry on the family name (Luke 1:7). The older brother in the parable of the prodigal son is addressed by his father, "My son [*teknon*] . . . everything I have is yours" (Luke 15:31 NIV). Acts 7:5 says that God promised Abraham the land "even though he had no *teknon*"—which here must refer to an heir. Paul can switch back and forth between *teknon* and *huios* in the same passage: "because those who are led by the Spirit of God are sons [*huioi*] of God. . . . The Spirit himself testifies with our spirit that we are God's children [*tekna*]. Now if we are children [*tekna*], then we are heirs—heirs of God and co-heirs with Christ. . . . The creation waits in eager expectation for the sons [*huioi*] of God to be revealed. . . . [T]he creation itself will be . . . brought into the glorious freedom of the children [*tekna*] of God" (Rom. 8:14, 16–17, 19, 21 NIV). Here the NIV consistently renders *huioi* by "sons" and *tekna* by "children," but it is difficult in the flow of this context to detect significant semantic distinction between the two terms. Note that *tekna* is closely tied to what it means to be an heir.

Once again, one must proceed case by case. But it is hard to avoid the conclusion that principle B.2 does not stand up very well to hard data.

CS Principle B.3

Finally, principle B.3 forbids translators from rendering the Hebrew and Greek words for "father" (ʾ*āb, patēr*) as "parent" or their respective plural forms (ʾ*ābôt, pateres*) as "ancestors." Once again, close inspection of every occurrence in the Old and New Testaments suggests there are some instances when a competent translator ought to do exactly what B.3 forbids. Thus Hebrews 11:23 RSV tells us, "By faith Moses, when he was born, was hid for three months by his *pateres*"—which here surely cannot be rendered as "fathers," but *must* be rendered as "parents." In Exodus 3:15 NRSV, Moses is told to tell the Israelites, "The LORD, the God of your ancestors [ʾ*ābôt*], . . . has sent me to you." The context suggests the reference is to many generations in the past, not the current range of "fathers." The word "ancestors" appears entirely suitable. Older versions usually have "fathers" here, but increasingly that is becoming an archaizing expression in such structures.

This is not to suggest thoughtless or wholesale transmutation of "father"/"fathers" into some inclusive-language alternative. Each passage must be examined carefully. It is to suggest that principle B.3 is too restrictive.[32]

But enough evaluation of the CBT and CS principles. To flesh things out a bit, I must venture a few more examples of various kinds. Such examples will occupy us for the next three short chapters.

6

SOME OLD TESTAMENT PASSAGES

Neither in this chapter nor in the next do I intend to break much fresh ground. Nevertheless, it might be useful to provide some brief comments on some more passages—in this chapter, passages from the Old Testament, and in the next, from the New Testament—to show how some of the linguistic and interpretive judgments articulated up to this point work out in practice. My comments here are brief; if the material from the previous chapters has not been absorbed, the arguments marshaled here may prove less than compelling.

More on Singulars and Plurals

We have already discussed this complicated issue somewhat. Because the English third-person singular pronoun is marked for gender ("he/she/it"), one of the expedients used by translators to avoid it is to switch to the plural, which is of course not marked for gender ("they"). Critics object that this loses the individualism implicit in the singular. I have argued that this is too univocal an explanation of the singular; that generic singulars abound; that passages must be assessed on a case-by-case basis, with the result that even if the criticism is judged valid in a particular passage, it does not necessarily follow that it is a compelling criticism in every passage where translators have rendered a Hebrew singular with an English plural.

In an unpublished paper, Professor John Stek has tracked not only the complex interplay of second- and third-person forms of address in regulative stipulations but also the strange shifting between singular and plural.[1] In this they are different from comparable ancient law codes; their form may owe rather more to suzerainty treaties, whether Hittite or Assyrian. For example, in the block of material that constitutes Exodus 20–23, the regulative instructions begin and end with second-person address. Third-person constructions are restricted to Exodus 21:1–22:20 (22:19 MT). But even this block *begins* with a second-person construction: "These are the laws you are to set before them: 'If *you* buy a Hebrew servant . . .' " (21:1–2 NIV). The collection of regulations found in the first major block of Leviticus has a similar interesting mix. "Speak to the Israelites [literally *sons of Israel*] and say to them, 'When any [*ʾādām*] of you [second-person masculine plural pronoun] brings an offering to the LORD, bring [second-person masculine plural verb] as your [second-person masculine plural pronoun] offering an animal from either the herd or the flock' " (Lev. 1:2 NIV)—which is then immediately followed by third-person masculine singular terminology that is syntactically controlled by the function of *ʾādām* in the verse just cited: "When an *ʾādām* of you brings an offering. . . . He is to. . . . He is to. . . ." Stek comments:

> Now given the facts noted above, viz., that the Pentateuch is made up of *public* documents that are regulative of the Yahweh-Israel covenant relationship and that in the ancient world *public* affairs were, with rare exception, the domain of the

men of the community, especially the heads of households, it is not surprising that 2nd-person language found in the regulative instructions is everywhere masculine. What is somewhat disconcerting for translators, at least initially, is the fact that in this literature no discriminating pattern can be shown in the use of the 2nd m. singular verbs and pronouns. The 2nd m. singular is used almost as freely for referring to the whole community of Israel as for referring to an individual.[2]

Some examples drive this home. The commandments of the Decalogue (Exod. 20:3–17) are all in second-person masculine singular form (though surely they were to be obeyed by men and women alike). But even the prologue (20:2) contains only second-person masculine singular constructions, even though these clearly refer to the entire covenant community. Again, observe the switching back and forth in the following passage (Exod. 34:11–16 NIV). All the commanding verbs are second-person singular except for those in italics (which are plural):

> Obey what I command you today. I will drive out before you the Amorites . . . and Jebusites. Be careful not to make a treaty with those who live in the land where you are going, or they will be a snare among you. *Break down* their altars, *smash* their sacred stones and *cut down* their Asherah poles. Do not worship any other god, for the LORD, whose name is Jealous, is a jealous God. Be careful not to make a treaty with those who live in the land; for . . . they will invite you and you will eat their sacrifices. And when you choose some of their daughters as wives for your sons and those daughters prostitute themselves to their gods, they will lead your sons to do the same.

By contrast, in Leviticus 19:23–37 all the second-person references are plural except those in 19:29, 32, and in the clause "Love him as yourself" (NIV) in verse 34 (though in Deut. 10:19 the verb is plural!). In Deuteronomy, the plural dominates, but one finds remarkable singulars in, for example, Deuteronomy 1:31; 2:24; 6:17.

Of course, as far as translation into English is concerned, contemporary English is marked for neither gender nor number in second-person imperative forms. By and large, translators have not felt it necessary to invent some device in English for preserving the constant number switches. Hebraists have long recognized the mismatch between Hebrew and English on such points, and have therefore not tried to preserve formal equivalences in English. Stek comments: "But even if such invention should be attempted, for example, 2nd-person pronominal forms [in English] that distinguished singular from plural, the distribution of these in accordance with Hebrew forms would leave the English reader who has no knowledge of the Hebrew merely perplexed. No *translation* gain would result."[3] Or, to use the language of linguists, the gender systems of the two languages are to some degree incommensurate, so to that degree the pursuit of formal equivalence is unhelpful. Where differences in form coincide with differences in semantics in *both* languages, of course, that is very helpful. But such coincidence must be demonstrated, not merely assumed.

Problems in Gender Changes

In the list of "problems in gender changes," a document prepared by Dr. John Piper with help from Dr. Wayne Grudem and presented to the group that met in Colorado Springs on May 27, 1997,[4] several Old Testament texts were mentioned. Those that are dealt with elsewhere in this book, either explicitly or implicitly, I need not mention again here. The remainder I shall now bring up in canonical order.

Numbers 8:17

NIV: "Every firstborn male in Israel, whether *man* or animal, is mine. When I struck down all the firstborn in Egypt, I set them apart for myself."

NIVI: "Every firstborn male in Israel, whether *human* or animal, is mine. When I struck down all the firstborn in Egypt, I set them apart for myself."

Dr. Piper lists this among the "gratuitous changes which mute obvious masculinity of persons," and asks, "Why give gender neutral translations to persons or groups that are obviously male?"[5]

I count Dr. Piper a good friend, and I admire his ministry. But I must say that this charge is misguided. Both the NIV and NIVI explicitly speak of "every firstborn male in Israel"; it is difficult to see how this "mutes" anyone's masculinity. But the "whether" phrase establishes the pool from which "every firstborn male in Israel" must be drawn: it includes both the human species and the (domestic) animal species. The NIVI is obviously superior. What is intriguing, however, is that Dr. Piper's insistence that the move from "man" to "human" mutes the maleness of the referent, however mistaken in this context, implicitly concedes what the NIVI and NRSV translators are constantly saying: the English word "man" often does have male overtones, even when the donor word, as here, does not. That is precisely why we need some gender-neutral translations.

Judges 18:7

NIV: "So the five *men* left and came to Laish."
NIVI: "So the five *of them* left and came to Laish."

Since the referent here is to warriors, and only under the most extraordinary circumstances were warriors women, there is no good reason to change from "men" to some gender-neutral form. Dr. Piper is right. Of course, the NIVI translation is not wrong in the sense that it is saying something false: it does not suggest that any of the warriors *were* women. Nevertheless, the change is unnecessary and leaves open a possibility that would have been culturally closed.

Psalm 19:11–12

NIV: "By them is your servant warned; in keeping them there is great reward. Who can discern *his* errors? Forgive my hidden faults."

NIVI: "By them is your servant warned; in keeping them there is great reward. Who can discern *their* errors? Forgive my hidden faults."

Dr. Piper observes that the change from "his" to "their" introduces a difficulty. There is only one obvious plural antecedent, namely, the ordinances of the Lord referred to by "them" in verse 11. One could read the NIVI to be saying that there are errors in God's ordinances.[6]

Dr. Piper is right, and the NRSV introduces the same unnecessary ambiguity. It appears that the translators, however laudable or otherwise their aim of producing a faithful gender-inclusive translation, have occasionally so focused their attention on this particular *desideratum* that they have introduced some glitches that need fixing. This is one of them. There are, of course, several ways around this. One could simply leave this masculine singular pronoun alone. One could paraphrase the offending line: "Who can discern your servant's errors?" A couple of other possibilities come to mind.

More Old Testament Examples

I turn to a list, in canonical order, of a number of other Old Testament passages that have been introduced into the discussion in various quarters.

Leviticus 18:5

NIV: "Keep my decrees and laws, for *the man* [*hā-ʾādām*] who obeys them will live by them."

NIVI: "Keep my decrees and laws, for *the one* who obeys them will live by them."

The NIVI is surely superior: the charge to keep God's decrees and laws is not laid on male human beings alone. If "man" increasingly has male overtones, the NIVI preserves a form of expression without that restriction. Similarly the NRSV; the NLT opts for "you."

Numbers 31:49

RSV: "Your servants have counted the *men* of war who are under our command, and there is *not a man* missing from us."

NRSV: "Your servants have counted the *warriors* who are under our command, and *not one* of us is missing."

See my comments above on Judges 18:7. The modern Israeli and American armies may be coed, but the ancient Israelite army wasn't. One or two colleagues have suggested that "warriors" has replaced "men of war" for no other reason than that the latter expression is obsolete. If they are right, then the NRSV is acceptable on these broader grounds. My own linguistic antennae, however, do not confirm that "men of war" is obsolete, and in any case the NRSV's bias is probably reflected in the shift from "not a man" to "not one."

Psalm 34:6

RSV: "This poor *man* cried, and the LORD heard him, and saved *him* out of all his troubles."

NRSV: "This poor *soul* cried, and was heard by the LORD, and was saved from every trouble."

Dr. Grudem objects that this fairly frequent device of the NRSV, the switch from an active to a passive voice in order to get rid of a troublesome pronoun, "doesn't tell us whether the person was saved by the Lord or by circumstances or by some other means. The Lord's salvation may be suggested by the NRSV, but it is not required, and the intended forcefulness of the text is lost. The Bible told us that the Lord saved him, but the NRSV no longer tells us. Once again, this is not translating the Bible; it is rewriting the Bible."[7]

I agree with Dr. Grudem's conclusion that the NRSV rendering is unacceptable, but for quite different reasons. Some languages do not have passives. Elegant Greek prefers passives (it is more colloquial Greek that opts for an abundance of actives); English usage reverses these priorities. In other words, just as gender systems differ from language to language, so also do voice systems. It cannot be a valid objection to a translation *in principle* that it opts for one voice when the donor has another: there are too many system factors that must be evaluated. That is the problem with translation. Of course, there may be legitimate objections to a change of voice in a particular location, even if there cannot be a legitimate objection to all changes of voice.

In this instance, I find the objection a bit strained. True, something of the vitality of the active is lost. But to suggest that the text does not make it clear that the Lord saved the "poor soul" who cried surely reflects leaden exegesis. Even the passive construction establishes that the "poor soul" was "heard *by the LORD,* and was saved." I cannot imagine a reader understanding this to mean (especially in the flow of this psalm) that this "poor soul" cried, was heard by the Lord, and then saved by circumstances quite apart from the Lord. That is bad reading, and the charge unfair. So far, the conclusion that the NRSV is here "rewriting the Bible" is unjustified; the charge reflects a failure to understand translation and its limitations.

Yet I entirely concur with Dr. Grudem's opinion that this is an unacceptable translation, because in this context the "poor man" is the psalmist. The superscription establishes who the author of this psalm is: none other than David.[8] There is nothing unseemly (in contemporary English) about David referring to himself as "this poor man." I note with gratitude that the NIVI here retains the wording of the NIV, presumably because it observes the context more carefully than does the

NRSV. Is it worth mentioning, in passing, that a weakness found in one gender-neutral translation does not necessarily condemn all gender-neutral translations?

Proverbs 5:1, 3, 7–8

Instead of "My son," these verses find a father addressing his child (in the NRSV): "My *child,* be attentive to my wisdom . . . for the lips of a loose woman drip honey, and her speech is smoother than oil. . . . And now, my *child,* listen to me. . . . Keep your way far from her, and do not go near the door of her house." Of course, many proverbs are addressed to men and women without exception. But here, warnings against being deceived by an adulteress make "son" far more likely to be a male than will generic labels for people of both sexes. The NIVI preserves "My son" throughout.

Proverbs 5:21

NIV: "For *a man's* ways are in full view of the LORD."
NIVI: "For *your* ways are in full view of the LORD."

Dr. Grudem objects that the NIVI "restricts the text to 'you,' who is the son being warned by his father in the previous text; the text no longer affirms God's observation of the ways of every person."[9] I find this unconvincing. The pronoun "you" can function, especially in aphorisms, much the way *on* does in French or *man* in German (compare "You get what you pay for"—which certainly does not mean the statement is true only for the "you" being addressed). To take the NIVI this way is surely unimaginative.

Proverbs 16:9

RSV: "A *man's* mind plans *his* way, but the LORD directs *his* steps."
NRSV: "The *human* mind plans *the* way, but the LORD directs *the* steps."

Dr. Grudem says it would have been appropriate to change the RSV to the following: "A *person's* mind plans his way, but the LORD directs his steps."[10] But this does not address the intrinsic limitation of English: only in the third-person singular is the pronoun marked for gender, and here that troublesome "his" resurfaces. One can, with Dr. Grudem, insist it is not a translation problem. But for those who believe it is, there are only so many ways around it. One could opt for the plural and drop "mind": "Human beings plan their ways, but the LORD directs their steps." I doubt that this would please him. In this instance, I rather favor the NIVI's move to the second person, because, as we have seen, "you" in English, especially in aphoristic contexts, can be appropriate for such utterances: "In your heart you may plan your course, but the LORD determines your steps." Compare comments on Proverbs 5:21, above.

Proverbs 29:3

NIV: "*A man* who loves wisdom brings joy to *his* father, but a companion of prostitutes squanders *his* wealth."

NIVI: "*Those* who love wisdom bring joy to *their* parents, but companions of prostitutes squander *their* wealth."

The person likely to visit prostitutes and squander wealth on them is a man. Here the NIVI falls into the same sort of trap as did the NRSV at Proverbs 5:1, 3, 7–8.

What is immediately obvious is that the critics of gender-inclusive translations of the Bible have sometimes administered some telling blows; at other times they appear to have missed the mark rather badly. At the risk of anticipating final conclusions, it appears that where the critics are right, they have not been so on the ground of a linguistically informed critique of gender-inclusive translations, but on the ground either of the CBT's occasional "loose" principle or of rather shoddy application now and then of the good guidelines that have been constructed. Where the critics have offered evaluations on the basis of an insecure linguistic foundation, they cannot be followed, even though we must thank them for exposing the more egregious mistakes that remain.

Incidentally, this sort of criticism is precisely why the original CBT of the NIV wanted to maintain the right to keep introducing corrections as they came in. But I have already wrestled with the problem of changing the text of a well-established Bible (see chapter 3, point 8 under "Implications and Conclusions").

It remains to assess some gender-inclusive renderings of New Testament passages.

7

SOME NEW TESTAMENT PASSAGES

In this chapter, as in the previous one, I do not intend to break much fresh ground. My purpose once again is to provide some brief comments on some more passages—in this chapter, from the New Testament—to show how some of the linguistic and interpretive principles articulated up to this point work out in practice. My comments are brief, as in chapter 6; if the material from chapters 1–5 has not been absorbed, the arguments here may not seem compelling.

Problems in Gender Changes

I shall begin with the New Testament references advanced by Dr. Piper in the paper he prepared for the May 27 meeting in Colorado Springs (mentioned in chapters 1 and 6), provided those references are not discussed elsewhere in this book.

Matthew 8:27

NIV: "The *men* were amazed and asked, 'What kind of man is this? Even the winds and the waves obey him!'"

> NIVI: "The *disciples* were amazed and asked, 'What kind of man is this? Even the winds and the waves obey him!'"

The Greek word is *anthrōpoi,* plural of *anthrōpos.* As explained in chapter 5 (under "CS Principles A.3, A.4, and A.5"), the most common meaning of the word is "human being," even when the referent is male (see also comments below on Acts 1:21). The trouble is that English does not use "human beings" or even "persons" or "people" in this sort of context to refer back to those whose identity has already been established. Since 8:23 specifies them to be disciples, the NIVI simply repeats the word in 8:27.

Whether this is wise may be disputed. If by "disciples" in 8:23 only the Twelve or some subset of them is meant, then the obvious word to use for *anthrōpoi* in 8:27 is "men" as in the NIV. But there is a not-uncommon uncertainty in the Synoptic Gospels as to whether "disciples" refers only to the Twelve or to some broader group of Jesus' followers. For instance, two verses before this pericope, a "disciple" asks Jesus a question that exposes the limitations of his discipleship. There is no reason whatsoever to think this was one of the Twelve. Certainly we know from elsewhere in the Gospels that women were included among the many who "followed" Jesus and who were "disciples" in that sense. The NIVI has apparently chosen to read 8:23–27 with the larger possibility kept open. In this case, their choice strikes me as unlikely, but I would be the first to concede that the evidence is not clear either way.

In short, in this instance I would have stayed with the NIV, but I cannot find sufficient evidence to warrant an attack on the NIVI.

Matthew 16:24–26

> NIV: "Then Jesus said to his disciples, '*If anyone* would come after me, *he* must deny *himself* and take up *his*

cross and follow me. For whoever wants to save *his life* will lose *it,* but *whoever loses his life* for me will find *it.* What good will it be for *a man* if *he* gains the whole world, yet forfeits *his* soul? Or what can *a man* give in exchange for *his* soul?'"

NIVI: "Then Jesus said to his disciples, '*Those who* would come after me must deny *themselves* and take up *their* cross and follow me. For *those who* want to save *their lives* will lose *them,* but *those who lose their lives* for me will find *them.* What good will it be for *you* to gain the whole world, yet forfeit *your* soul? Or what can *you* give in exchange for *your* soul?'"

Dr. Piper comments that in the NIVI "the individual thrust and personal responsibility of Jesus' words are lessened in this plural rendering, and the change from 'a man' to 'you' may give the impression that it relates to Jesus' hearers rather than being a universal statement."[1] I have repeatedly responded to these objections (see chapters 5 and 6) and will not repeat all the arguments again. Suffice it to say that formal plurals often have personal application *intended* by the speaker/writer and picked up by ordinary readers (for example, Matt. 5:6, 10); that "you" not infrequently has the value in English of a French *on* or a German *man,* and does not strike me in this context as restrictive in the way suggested by Dr. Piper; that in this instance the suggestion that "personal responsibility" is lessened by the switch to the plural is in any case overturned by the "you," which if anything increases "personal responsibility."

Many of the texts adduced by the critics of all gender-inclusive translations are of this type. The question behind the question is invariably the same: Granted the current trends in English usage, should an attempt be made to find an alternative construction to the third-person singular pronoun, which in English is marked for gender, wherever the *meaning* of the original is not gender-restrictive? If the answer is no, then no change is necessary or helpful. If the answer is yes, then it is not enough to say that you do not like the alternatives to "he" and related pronouns, no matter what they are. That is the perennial problem with all translations: you must use the structures of the receptor language to convey the meaning you find in the donor language, even though the structures of the two languages are sufficiently different that you are forced into over-specification and under-specification and so forth.[2]

So I shall not return to more of these kinds of texts, since the answers will always be the same. The only exceptions will be where additional factors come into play (as in John 14:23; Gal. 5:10; Rev. 3:20, below).

John 11:50

> NIV: "it is better for you that one *man* [*anthrōpos*] die for the people than that the whole nation perish."
>
> NIVI: "it is better for you that one *person* die for the people than that the whole nation perish."

A similar change occurs at John 18:14. Compare also 1 Corinthians 15:21:

> NIV: "For since death came through a *man* [*anthrōpos*], the resurrection of the dead comes also through a *man*."
>
> NIVI: "For since death came through a *human being,* the resurrection of the dead comes also through a *human being*."

Dr. Piper views these as an instances in which the "masculinity of Jesus is downplayed."[3] This is a repeat of the misconception advanced by Dr. Köstenberger regarding Philippians 2:8, 1 Timothy 2:5, and similar passages (see chapter 5 under "CS Principles A.3, A.4, and A.5"). This is not "downplaying" Jesus' masculinity; it is faithfully translating into current English the primary meaning of *anthrōpos*. At no point does the NIVI deny Jesus' masculinity. The fact remains that Jesus was not only a male, he was a human male. Throughout the history of the church, theologians have wrestled with how best to articulate the simultaneous truths that Jesus was truly "God" and truly "man"—with "man" in such discourse meaning "human being." That he was a *particular* "man" (that is, human being) was also affirmed—a male human with a particular first-century Jewish identity, the son of Mary, and so forth. But the primary focus of theological integration was how simultaneously to affirm Jesus' deity and his humanity.

When referring to Jesus' humanity, the word "man" (in English-language theological discussion) was universally used. Adam also was of course a male human being. As for 1 Corinthians 15:21, the question is whether the choice of language here emphasizes his maleness or his humanness. Lexically, *anthrōpos* primarily means "human being"; theologically, that entirely fits this context. Through Adam's sin, death came upon all human beings; it was Adam's role as federal head of the human race that was critical.

Not only is the NIVI's translation not pernicious, but Dr. Piper unwittingly concedes the very point that the NIVI translators and others are trying to make. Saying that the change from "man" to "person" or "human being" downplays Jesus' masculinity presupposes that the word "man" is tied to maleness, to masculinity. At one time it could be used in a purely generic sense, and virtually all readers would take it that way. If Dr. Piper had argued that "man" still has this sense unambiguously and a change to "human being" is therefore unnecessary, then we could argue about whether or not the English language has changed (see chapter 9). But by arguing that the move away from "man" reduces Jesus' masculinity, Piper concedes that even for him "man" does not here carry gender-neutral reference to "person" or "human being"—which is precisely what *anthrōpos* here *does* mean. Granted such (unwitting) concessions, I insist that the NIVI is in this case more accurate than the NIV, not because we are changing the

Word of God or rewriting it, but because the English language is changing such that older translations sometimes give a false impression that gender-neutral translations actually correct. This is not to say that the NIVI or NRSV is always right; I have criticized some of their renderings and will criticize others. It is to say that some of the critics' charges are too sweeping or sadly misjudged.

John 14:23

NIV: "If *anyone loves* me, he will obey my teaching. My Father will love *him,* and we will come to *him* and make our home with *him.*"

NIVI: "*Those who* love me will obey my teaching. My Father will love *them,* and we will come to *them* and make our home with *them.*"

The implication in the change, charge the critics, is that Jesus and the Father dwell "with a group rather than with a person."[4] In this case the critics have a point. I have earlier argued, several times, that the move from the singular to the plural in most instances entails very little loss of individual application: many plurals in English work that way anyway. But in this case there is an additional factor, an important one. In the New Testament, "Jesus" or "God" or the "Holy Spirit" entertains relations with, or lives in or dwells with, sometimes the believing community and sometimes the individual believer. This is one of the passages which, in Greek, clearly tilts to the latter. Because the more corporate emphasis is well known, a shift to the plural may make some readers, especially those more theologically informed but with no knowledge of the original languages, suppose that once again the corporate sense is found in the original. On balance, therefore, the criticism in this instance is sound.

What to do about it is another matter. It is always important to remember the limitations of translation and to walk humbly. Still, in this instance, there are several options apart from the alternatives offered by the NIV and NIVI. Of course, one might simply leave the NIV in place, perhaps with an explanatory note (as the NRSV in one or two places finds no graceful way out of gender-specific language in English that is not really mandated by the original, but leaves it that way because of the limitations of the receptor language). There are other options.

Acts 1:21

> NIV: "Therefore it is necessary to choose one *of the men* who have been with us the whole time the Lord Jesus went in and out among us."
>
> NIVI: "Therefore it is necessary to choose one *of those* who have been with us the whole time the Lord Jesus went in and out among us."

The word for "of the men" (NIV) is *andrōn,* the genitive plural of *anēr.* We saw in chapter 5 (under "CS Principles A.3, A.4, and A.5") that *anthrōpos* normally means "human being," though its referent is often male—sometimes incidentally so and sometimes crucially so. By contrast, *anēr* most commonly means "man" (that is, male human being) or "husband." There are some remarkable exceptions where even this word *must* be understood to include both men and women, but they are relatively rare.

In this context, I see no reason for removing the reference to men. That is the "default" understanding of *anēr,* here strengthened by the fact that the issue is replacing one of the Twelve, all of whom were males, the two suggested replacements likewise being male.

Galatians 5:10

> NIV: "The one who is throwing you into confusion will pay the penalty, whoever *he* may be."

NIVI: "The one who is throwing you into confusion will pay the penalty, whoever *that* may be."

Dr. Piper sees this as one of the "gratuitous changes," and I agree with him.[5] In the context, the individual here referred to, whether a kind of collective singular or not, certainly belongs to those "agitators" whom Paul, two verses later, wishes would go all the way and "emasculate themselves" (5:12). It is hard not to grin and conclude that the CBT got carried away with its guidelines and did not keep its collective eye on the context.

Revelation 3:20

NIV: "Here I am! I stand at the door and knock. If anyone hears my voice and opens the door, I will come in and eat with *him,* and *he* with me."

NIVI: "Here I am! I stand at the door and knock. If anyone hears my voice and opens the door, I will come in and eat with *them,* and *they* with me."

Dr. Piper objects that "the grammatically inconsistent transition between 'anyone' and 'them . . . they' obscures the personal relationship with Christ offered in this verse."[6] True, this construction is "grammatically inconsistent." I do not much care for it—but then I am enough of a traditionalist that I do not much like "It's me" either, which is equally grammatically inconsistent and now almost universally judged acceptable. As for obscuring the personal relationship, I find this mistaken not only on the general ground repeatedly mentioned in this book—that quite demonstrably many grammatical plurals carry an individual application that is recognized by all but the most unperceptive readers—but also on the ground that the "grammatical inconsistency" preserves the "anyone." Incidentally, the NRSV here tackles the gender-specific pronoun by switching to the second person: "Listen! I am standing at the door, knocking; if you hear my voice and open the door, I will come in to you and eat with *you,* and *you* with me.'"[7]

More New Testament Examples

We may now pick up on a number of other New Testament verses that have been introduced into the discussion. Once again, this list is not exhaustive. By and large I do not here treat verses I have discussed elsewhere in this book.

Luke 17:3

NIV: "If your *brother* sins, rebuke him, and if *he* repents, forgive *him*."

NIVI: "Rebuke a *brother or sister* who sins, and if *they* repent, forgive *them*."

Dr. Grudem comments: "Trying to make 'they' singular impoverishes English by leaving us no clearly plural pronoun; but understanding 'they' as plural mistranslates the singular Greek pronoun *autos* and corresponding singular verb. (And the lack of agreement in many verses like this creates dissonant English as well.) Jesus could easily have said 'brother or sister' if he had wanted to (see 1 Corinthians 7:15)."[8]

It is difficult to respond to this series of criticisms without referring to the whole of this book so far written. To use "they" this way, Dr. Grudem suggests, "impoverishes English." But the point is that English is already impoverished by not having a gender-neutral third-person singular pronoun. Languages are constantly going through changes of one sort or another, driven by various factors: shall we insist on using archaisms so as not to "impoverish" the language? Shall we continue to use "thou" and related forms because by dropping them we have "impoverished" the English language by losing a clear distinction between second-person singular and second-person plural forms? In any case we do not thereby lose power to communicate: spoken language is a living thing and finds ways to get across *needed* distinctions.[9]

But the deeper problem with Dr. Grudem's analysis is that it assumes that the gender and number relationships internal to contemporary English are exactly the same as in Greek. To speak of what the NIVI has done here as "mistranslation" betrays an unfortunate misapprehension about how languages relate to one another, and therefore how translation works. In the revised form of the CSG, as we have seen, Dr. Grudem and his colleagues now rightly concede that sometimes "brothers" in Greek may include both "brothers and sisters." The same is true (I argued in chapter 5 under "CS Principle B.1") of the singular "brother" in Greek. This does not mean that *every* instance of "brothers" has this larger compass; it does mean that the context must be evenhandedly examined, for it is extraordinarily rare that the entire semantic range of a word is carried by that word when it is in syntactical flow. As the word shapes the context, so the context shapes the word. Having admitted that "brothers" in Greek can in the right context mean "brothers and sisters," Dr. Grudem must also surely see that Luke or Paul or any other New Testament writer *could* have written "brothers and sisters" (and sometimes did so), even though that same writer might choose on occasion to write "brothers" and thereby mean what we mean when we say "brothers and sisters." In other words, there may be such semantic overlap between "brothers" and "brothers and sisters" that *in certain contexts* the two expressions mean the same thing. Similarly here: for exactly the same reasons, the statement "Jesus could easily have said 'brother or sister' if he had wanted to" is of course correct—and entirely without weight in this particular argument.

John 11:25

NIV: "Jesus said to her, 'I am the resurrection and the life. *He* who believes in me will live, even though *he* dies.' "

NIVI: "Jesus said to her, 'I am the resurrection and the life. *Those* who believe in me will live, even though *they* die.' "

Dr. Grudem says that the forcefulness of the promise to an individual person is lost and that the text "mistranslates" four singular Greek words. Then he adds in parentheses: "Note that Jesus did not hesitate to use generic 'he' even when speaking to Martha."

I have already said more than enough to question the argument about the "forcefulness of promise" to the "individual person." Here it is what is in parentheses that draws our attention. True, in one sense we may argue that "Jesus did not hesitate to use generic 'he' even when speaking to Martha"—in precisely what sense we shall see in a moment. On the radio program *Open Line* (May 13, 1997), Dr. Grudem argues with Dr. Kenneth Barker along the same lines: Why should a woman be offended by such language today? If she lived in Jesus' day, would she have been offended? And in any case, this is the terminology that Jesus used: he chose the generic singular "he," even when talking with a woman.[10] Martha was apparently not offended; why therefore does any woman have the right to be offended today?

But again, this line of argument entirely misses the point. True, Jesus (in John's report) did use the *Greek* generic "he." He also used genitive absolutes, double accusatives compounded with aorist infinitives, double negatives, and a host of other constructions all of which would be either incomprehensible or seriously misleading if rendered into English by a merely formal equivalent. In this instance, Jesus did *not* use generic "he"; he used generic *autos*. Precisely because it was understood to be generic, it could not cause "offense" (though in my view that is not the primary issue at stake) or incomprehension precisely because Martha understood the pronoun in this context to be broad enough in its semantic range to include her. Similarly if a modern woman went back in time to that culture with a profound grasp of the language and literature of that culture, she would be unlikely to take umbrage. But if "he" in English, complete with gender specification, is used in a generic sense somewhat less frequently than it used to be, and if for some sections of the reading populace "he" is never or almost never used in a generic sense anymore, then fidelity to the original demands the choice of an expression that is less formally proximate, or we lose some part of what the original text says.

If Dr. Grudem wishes instead to argue that "he" still has enough generic force in a sufficiently large part of the English world to retain use of that pronoun in this context, he is at perfect liberty to do so—indeed, that is in effect precisely what he argues when he adduces instances where generic "he" still operates. I shall come to that question in chapter 9. But he is not at liberty to use the form of argument he has inserted in his parenthesis here. That confuses receptor and donor languages and betrays a misconception as to the relationships between languages and therefore of the nature of translation. On the long haul that sort of argument can only lessen the credibility of the valid points of criticism he offers with respect to some passages, to which I have already referred.

Acts 9:7

> NIV: "The *men* traveling with Saul stood there speechless; they heard the sound but did not see anyone."
>
> NIVI: "*Those* who were travelling with Saul stood there speechless; they heard the sound but did not see anyone."

The Greek is *andres,* plural for *anēr,* and as in Acts 1:21, one should assume the reference is to male human beings, unless there is convincing contextual counter-evidence. Here Dr. Köstenberger is right in his objection to the NIVI translation.[11]

Acts 20:30

NIV: "Even from your own number *men* will arise and distort the truth in order to draw away disciples after them."

NIVI: "Even from your own number *some* will arise and distort the truth in order to draw away disciples after them."

Dr. Grudem charges that this change "obliterates the fact that Paul used a specific Greek noun *andres* [plur. of *anēr*] to say that the false teachers coming at Ephesus would be 'men'; this word never refers to women, and 'some' is a mistranslation."[12] I imagine Dr. Grudem wrote these lines before the revision of the CS principles. Revised principle A.4 says that *anēr* should "almost always" be rendered "man" (or "men" in the plural). That is correct (see the discussion in chapter 5 under "CS Principles A.3, A.4, and A.5"). With Dr. Grudem, I do not see any warrant for changing the NIV's "men" in this passage, even though his claim that *anēr* "never refers to women" is quite demonstrably too strong. Moreover, since Paul is at this point addressing the elders at Ephesus, and there is no convincing textual evidence that New Testament elders included women (as there is, by contrast, convincing evidence that New Testament deacons included women), it is prejudicial to hint otherwise.

I Corinthians 13:11

NIV: "When I became a *man* [*anēr*], I put childish ways behind me."

NIVI: "When I became an *adult,* I put childish ways behind me."

This change is silly. Paul grew up to become a man, a male human being. Someone might reply, "Yes, but aren't you now being inconsistent? Elsewhere (in chapter 5 under 'CS Principles A.3, A.4, and A.5') you say that sometimes a Greek word has the *meaning* of 'human being' while it *refers* to a man. Couldn't the same thing be said here?" No, because the word in chapter 5 with which I was dealing was *anthrōpos*; here it is *anēr*. The two words *can* occupy the same semantic space in specific contexts. But as we have seen, the "default" meaning of the former is "human being"; you need a good reason to think that maleness is being conveyed. Precisely the opposite is the case with the latter word: a male human being is normally in view, and you need a good contextual reason to extend beyond that restriction.

I Corinthians 14:28

NIV: "If there is no interpreter, the speaker should keep quiet in the church and speak to *himself* and God."

NIVI: "If there is no interpreter, the speakers should keep quiet in the church and speak to *themselves* and God."

Dr. Grudem says the change could "easily be understood to encourage groups of tongue-speakers to go off together and speak in tongues 'to themselves.'" Moreover, the NIVI "[m]istranslates three singular Greek words which Paul wrote."

I need not respond again to the charge of "mistranslation" of three Greek words: the same fundamental misconceptions are still operating. But Dr. Grudem's first point is worth thinking about. In most instances, I have argued, the change of single person to plural in a moralizing or ethical context entails no loss: English-speaking readers apply such texts personally anyway. Here and there, however, I have argued that the critics may have a point because of (1) the peculiar way that the English plural functions in a specific context or (2) the odd overtones it carries there. See, for example, my comments on John 14:23, above. Here Dr. Grudem has put his finger on another instance when the plural can be misleading: granted contemporary practice, it is quite possible that some tongues-speakers might understand the plural rendering of the NIVI as sanction "to go off together and speak in tongues 'to themselves.'" It might be better to find another alternative or include an explanatory note.

Titus 1:6

According to Dr. Grudem, "Paul tells Titus to appoint elders in Crete who meet the criterion, 'the *husband* [*anēr*] of one wife' (Titus 1:6, RSV), but NRSV translates, 'married only once' (NRSV), which of course could include women elders as well as men."[13] Dr. Grudem then advances various arguments. With Dr. Grudem, I doubt that the peculiar Greek expression means "married only once" anyway. But moreover, that stubborn *anēr* is used here, and must not be ignored. The NIVI renders the phrase "the husband of but one wife."[14]

James 1:12

NIV: "Blessed is the *man* who perseveres under trial, because when *he* has stood the test, *he* will receive the crown of life."

NIVI: "Blessed are *those* who persevere under trial, because when *they* have stood the test, *they* will receive the crown of life."

Several have objected to the NIVI rendering, partly because behind the word "man" is Greek *anēr*. Dr. Köstenberger is especially hard on those who opt for any rendering of this Greek word other than "man."[15] But in chapter 5 (under "CS Principles A.3, A.4, and A.5") I tried to show convincing evidence that although *anēr* most commonly means "man," that is, male human being, nevertheless both in the lexica and in texts some extension is occasionally found. In this instance, is James really saying that only male human beings are blessed if they persevere under trial? If one responds that he is using the male to refer to both men and women, one is already conceding that the word *in this context* demands a rendering that is similarly comprehensive. Indeed, although I would not go to the stake for it, I am almost prepared to say that in the peculiar idiolect of James, *anēr* in his usage functions the way *anthrōpos* does among other writers.

I Peter 3:4

To put some things in perspective, I include this last example. It is important to remember that the passage in question is talking about Christian wives and about that in which their beauty consists.

> KJV: "But let it be the *hidden man* [*anthrōpos*] of the heart, in that which is not corruptible, even the ornament of a meek and quiet spirit."
>
> NIV/NIVI: "Instead, it should be that of your *inner self,* the unfading beauty of a gentle and quiet spirit."

As Kohlenberger says, "I don't want my wife to have a 'hidden man of the heart.' It might be the premise for a modern sitcom, but it's not a mandate for biblical femininity."[16]

Many more passages could usefully be explored, but one must draw the line somewhere. In these two chapters (chapters 6 and 7), my aim has been, building out of the linguistic and translation theory of the previous chapters, to consider a select number of passages from the Old and New Testaments in order to determine how valid are the charges leveled against inclusive-language translations. At the risk of a simplistic summary when the data themselves are enormously complex, it appears that the critics have scored some points in particular passages (and in others that have not been discussed), and the CBT should take the most telling of these criticisms seriously and be even more careful in the future than they have been. We can all learn from one another. On the other hand, the sweep of the criticisms against the NIVI and other gender-inclusive translations will not stand. The undergirding understanding of language and translation (and occasionally even exegesis) is sufficiently flawed that the attack will not long prove successful or widely convincing.

Before we leave these examples, however, I should devote a few pages to passages where some of the most important doctrinal issues are raised in debate.

8

SOME CRITICAL PASSAGES WITH IMPORTANT DOCTRINAL ISSUES AT STAKE

There is a sense, of course, in which the entire discussion of this book carries with it important doctrinal issues: we do not have to wait for this chapter before coming upon important doctrines. The critics of the NIVI and other gender-inclusive English versions are doubtless motivated by the highest concerns to preserve the truth of Scripture and to treat God's words with respect: that itself is a doctrinal matter. We have already had reason to reflect on whether several passages refer to Jesus as a "human being" or as a "man," that is, a male human being: certainly it is difficult to think of topics more important than Christology. So not for a moment am I suggesting that the limited number of topics I shall briefly comment on in this short chapter constitute the only important doctrinal issues in the debate.

But what sets the following few issues apart is the intertwining of linguistic/translational matters with theological factors sufficiently complex that we find ourselves comparing several passages and evaluating several themes at once. Each of these issues could easily call forth a book. Nevertheless, a few paragraphs each may help to clarify some of these matters.

Adam and the Human Race

The issues are complex. Consider, first, two passages, in various translations:

Genesis 1:26–27

KJV: "And God said, 'Let us make *man* [*ʾādām*] in our image, after our likeness: and let *them* have dominion. . . .' So God created *man* [*hā-ʾādām*] in his own image, in the image of God created he *him*; male and female created he *them*."

NASB: "And God said, 'Let us make *man* in our image, according to our likeness; and let *them* rule. . . .' And God created *man* in His own image, in the image of God He created *him*; male and female He created *them*."

NIV: "Then God said, 'Let us make *man* in our image, in our likeness, and let *them* rule. . . .' So God created *man* in his own image, in the image of God he created *him*; male and female he created *them*."

NIVI: "Then God said, 'Let us make *human beings* in our image, in our likeness, and let *them* rule. . . .' So God created *human beings* in his own image, in the image of God he created *them*; male and female he created *them*."

Genesis 5:1–3

KJV: "This is the book of the generations of *Adam* [*ʾādām*]. In the day that God created *man* [*ʾādām*], in the likeness of God made he *him*; male and female he created *them*; and blessed *them,* and called *their* name *Adam* [*ʾādām*], in the day when *they* were created. And *Adam* [*ādām*] lived an hundred and thirty years, and begat a son in *his* own likeness, after *his* image; and called his name Seth."

NIV: "This is the written account of *Adam's* line. When God created *man,* he made *him* in the likeness of God. He created *them* male and female and blessed *them.* And when *they* were created, he called them '*man.*'[1] When *Adam* had lived 130 years, *he* had a son in *his* own likeness, in *his* own image; and *he* named him Seth."

NIVI: "This is the written account of *Adam's* line. When God created *human beings,* he made *them* in the likeness of God. He created *them* male and female and blessed *them.* And when *they* were created, he called them '*human beings.*'[2] When *Adam* had lived 130 years, *he* had a son in *his* own likeness, in *his* own image; and *he* named him Seth."

Principle A.3 of the CSG asserts that "'man' should ordinarily be used to designate the human race," giving as examples of such texts, among others, Genesis 1:26–27 and 5:2. Dr. Grudem contends:

> The name "man" is placed on both male and female, as together they constitute the human race. The translation "man" is accurate, because the Hebrew word *ʾādām* is also used to refer to Adam in particular, and it is sometimes used to refer to man in distinction from woman (see Gen. 2:25, "the man and his wife were both naked, and were not ashamed"). The English word "man" most accurately translates *ʾādām* because it is the only word we have that has those same two meanings (the human race, or a male human being). We can conclude from this usage of *ʾādām* that it is not wrong, insensitive, or discourteous to use the same word to refer to male human beings in particular and to name the human race. God himself does this in his Word. . . .
>
> . . . The problem is that "humankind," "human beings," and "human" are not names that can also refer to man in distinc-

tion from woman, and thus they are a less accurate translations [*sic*] of *ʾādām* than the word "man." The male overtones
of the Hebrew word are lost.[3]

Dr. Grudem is partly right: it would be nice to use an English
word that would cover both senses, namely, the human race
and the male of the human race. But as the quotations above
indicate, what is really required is not a word that will include
only these two senses, but one that will include a third as well,
namely, the proper name "Adam."

That's the problem, and it is not minor. In some passages
in the opening chapters of Genesis, there is considerable dispute as to precisely when *ʾādām* is to be understood as a proper
name and when it refers to the human race as a whole.[4] That
surfaces, for instance, in Genesis 5:2: contrast the KJV and NIV.
Did God call the race "Adam" or "man"? In fact, versions variously opt for "Adam" (KJV), "Man" (ASV, NASB, JB), "man"
(NEB, NIV, REB), "Humankind" (NRSV), "human beings" (CEV).
Strictly speaking, of course, God called it *ʾādām*. Our problem is that "Adam" represents a transliteration of the Hebrew
word (that is, we merely spell it in letters as close as possible
in sound to the Hebrew letters and try to pronounce it more
or less the same way as in Hebrew), whereas "man" and any
of the other renderings are not transliterations but translations.

So we have already lost one of the three uses of *ʾādām* in
these chapters (its use as a proper name), no matter what we
do. Of course, strictly speaking both the NIV and NIVI, by their
footnote in 5:2, try to preserve something of the connection.
Shall we then insist on maintaining "man" because two out
of three is better than one out of three?

There is something to be said for that view. That was in fact
the practice, in English, until very recently. (Of course, in
some languages even this is not possible: some languages have
different words for "man" [that is, male human being] and
"humankind.") In part the question is whether or not "man"
in English is becoming so restrictively male that it does not

function well in the two semantic slots that Dr. Grudem wants to assign it. Of course, he will deny that "man" is no longer suitable; I will merely say that in my view the language is changing, and for at least some readers "man" is no longer the best word to use to render *ʾādām* when the Hebrew word is referring to the human race. Once again, I must postpone discussion until chapter 9.

One way out, of course, is to include more notes to draw attention to the Hebrew word and its range, right through these chapters, and regardless of what option is finally chosen. Another option is, along with the notes, to preserve "man" here, and then use other words in most of the other biblical passages where people of both sexes are referred to. But that too will demand some lengthy explanatory notes.

There are other complicating factors. In Hebrew *ʾādām* has no plural. If one explicitly wishes to pluralize it, one resorts to *bĕnê ʾādām* (literally "sons of Adam"). But when *ʾādām* is used absolutely, it may refer to the individual whom we call "Adam" or even in a few instances to some other individual male human being (Gen. 16:12; Lev. 16:17; Josh. 14:15; Neh. 2:10; Eccles. 7:28). *Everywhere* else, however, out of a total of 562 occurrences in the Old Testament, the word refers either to the human race as corporate race or to human beings generally. In other words, the overwhelming preponderance of usage is generic, and frequently collective. Yet because the form of the word is singular, some strange wobbles in the number of the related pronouns are introduced (as is clear even from the quotations above). Consider, for instance, Psalm 84:4–5 (84:5–6 MT): "Blessed are *those* [plural] who dwell in your house; *they* [plural] are ever praising you. Blessed is *ʾādām whose* [singular] strength is in you, in *whose* [plural] heart are pilgrimages" (author's translation). Clearly, the collective singular *ʾādām* can control either a singular or a plural pronoun. Or again, Jonah 4:11: "And should I not spare Nineveh, that great city, wherein are more than sixscore thousand *persons* [*ʾādām*] that cannot discern between *their* [masculine singular pronoun] right hand and *their* [masculine singular pronoun] left hand; and also much cattle?" (KJV). Try and maintain formal equivalence in a passage like that!

One must also point out that in the Hebrew Bible, the names of other progenitors of "tribes" can function the same way. Moab is the father of the Moabites, Edom (Esau) of the Edomites, and Israel of the Israelites. In each case the word can refer to the individual, or it may be a collective. When it carries a collective sense, it can control either singular or plural pronouns.[5]

As for the importance of "naming" things, in Genesis 1–3 God "names" or "calls" other things besides *ʾādām:* day, night, heavens/sky, earth/land, and so forth. By contrast, he assigns to Adam the responsibility to "name" or "call" all the creatures God brings before him. Thus a distinction is drawn between God's overarching sovereignty over the whole of creation, and the peculiar sphere of relative sovereignty that God assigns to his image bearer.

Space constraints forbid a detailed analysis of Genesis 2, where eventually the author of Genesis moves from *hā-ʾādām* to *ʾîsh.* Other factors could be introduced: is this issue tied to Christology, that is, to "new Adam Christology"? But my point is that the matter is clearly complex. Dr. Grudem's case has some merit; I do not think it is a black-and-white issue, however, for it is more complex than he allows, and the balance of judgments, in my view, comes out a different way.

Son of Man

Principle A.9 of the CSG asserts that "the phrase 'son of man' should ordinarily be preserved to retain intracanonical connections." At the same time, there has been strenuous objection to the ninety or so instances of "mortal" instead of "son of man" in God's address to Ezekiel in the NRSV (the NIVI retains "son of man"). But the biggest issue is that while "Son of Man" is one of the commonest messianic titles of Jesus, its

Old Testament roots are obscured if the title is preserved in the New Testament (which is what all the gender-inclusive translations do) while obliterating the expression in the Old Testament by hiding it under "mortal" or "human being" or something else.

I shall offer six brief reflections.

1. No one doubts that "son of man" *(ben-ʾādām)* means "human being" in the Old Testament. In modern Hebrew, it still does. Similarly, the plural *bĕnê ʾādām* means "human beings." Moreover, chapter 5 (under "CS Principles A.3, A.4, and A.5") provides parallels in Job where the expression is clearly parallel to one of the other Hebrew words for human being. So *in part* we have stumbled again into the tension between form and meaning.

2. The expression is unambiguously Semitic. The Greek equivalent, *ho huios tou anthrōpou,* sounds almost as strange in Greek as "the son of man" does in contemporary English. That is one of the reasons why the expression is retained in translations of the New Testament. The second reason, of course, is that it is a christological title with a range of meanings *beyond* mere "human being."

3. Not every Old Testament passage with *ben-ʾādām* in it is messianic. See, for instance, the parallels in chapter 5 (under "CS Principles A.3, A.4, and A.5"). The NIV therefore often rendered the Hebrew expression "sons of men" by "men"[6] or by "mankind."[7] It follows that principle A.9 is too narrow.

4. The most obvious Old Testament antecedent to "son of man" as a christological title for Jesus is Daniel 7:13–14:

In my vision at night I looked, and there before me was *one like a son of man,* coming with the clouds of heaven. He approached the Ancient of Days and was led into his presence. He was given authority, glory and sovereign power; all peoples, nations and men of every language worshiped him. (NIV, emphasis mine)

The NRSV has "one like a human being," with a footnote that reads: "Aram[aic] *one like a son of man.*" The NIVI, by contrast, preserves "one like a son of man" in the text, and in its footnote reads: "Or *a human being.*"

In one sense, this is yet another instance of the tension between meaning and form. The Hebrew or Aramaic expression "son of man" *means* human being: on that point there is virtually no disagreement. But because the expression, rendered formally into Greek and then into English, has become in its application to Jesus Christ almost a technical term and certainly an established title, in this case the form must be preserved, or something important is lost at the level of canonical coherence. So I prefer the NIVI to the NRSV at this point.

When the NRSV first appeared, I criticized it on this point, and was told by one of the Old Testament scholars on their committee that "son of man" really *means* "human being" and they were after *meaning,* and that in any case it would have been wrong to ignore the sensibilities of the Jewish scholars on the NRSV committee. Subsequently I responded in print, saying that ironically I agreed with both points.[8] I never doubted that "son of man" *means* "human being." Moreover, translations should *not* needlessly offend the sensibilities of readers, whether Jewish, African American, conservative Christians, women, or whatever. Of course, sometimes those two goals clash! But in any case my point was a technical one. "From the translator's point of view, the question to be considered in this case is the instrument by which the translation should preserve the linguistic *form* of an expression so that the appropriate inner-biblical link can be spotted by someone without access to the original languages."[9] As for Jewish sensibilities, one must frankly recognize that Jewish and Christian communities do not share exactly the same canon. Bibles are attached to communities. Translations that cross communities usually make gains in terms of fairness and rigor,[10] but there may be losses as well. In this case, at least some Jewish scholars interested in, say, "son of man" in the "Similitudes" of 1 Enoch might also have an interest in preserving the linguistic *form* of the expression in Daniel 7.

5. A further question is how many other Old Testament passages with "son of man" in them should preserve the form, on the ground that they too provide something of the necessary background to the title applied to Jesus. That is an extraordinarily difficult question to answer. Some would immediately adduce Psalm 8, but there I remain unconvinced: see the next section, below. The difficulty resides in the fact that even if not one Old Testament passage is explicitly picked up in the New Testament technical term "son of man," the constant use of the expression in the Old Testament to refer to a human being is precisely what lends some of the ambiguity to Jesus' use of it. When Jesus applies "son of man" to himself, on many occasions it means very little more than "I" (as a perusal of the Synoptic parallels attests). In some contexts there are overtones of weakness and impending death; in others the reference is unambiguously to the apocalyptic "son of man" coming on the clouds of heaven (Mark 14:62). But if the only "son of man" that is preserved in the Old Testament *in this form* is the apocalyptic figure of Daniel 7, then the basis for the ambiguity on which Jesus' use relies is largely dissolved.

As cumbersome as it is, therefore, on the whole I favor a retention of "son of man," at least in the majority of its Old Testament occurrences, and probably with a brief note to accompany most of them. The exceptions might be (for instance) some of the occurrences in the poetical wisdom literature.

At this point it is worth reflecting for a moment on the different approaches I have advocated for "son of man" and "sons of Israel." In the former case a wider preservation of the (English translation of the) form, and not merely the meaning, is defensible; in the latter, there is no particular merit in retaining the form, so long as the meaning is preserved. Why the difference? The reason, of course, is because the New Testament Greek translation of the Hebrew and Aramaic form of "son of man" is preserved, and that form has come down to us in English, regardless of how "un-English" it is—and this form has itself become reified in Christian Scripture to a christological title. So an additional theological and historical wrinkle has been added to the challenge of translating this particular expression.

Here the NIVI has been more sensitive than the NRSV. In pursuit of gender-neutral English, the NRSV becomes monofocal and sometimes forgets that other issues are at stake beyond merely linguistic matters. One may question the NIVI judgments here and there (as I have), but by and large the CBT translators are more sensitive to these additional factors than their counterparts behind the NRSV. If the critics of gender-neutral versions have forced us to reflect on some of these matters more carefully, then even if we disagree profoundly with their approach to language and translation, we may be grateful to God, and to them, for helping us to go about this business of translation more prudently and with wider horizons.

6. Finally, we must probe the wisdom of rendering "son of man" by "mortal." The NRSV is especially lavish in its use of this term as a replacement of "man" or "men" or "son of man": for example, "*O mortal* [literally, 'son of man'], stand up on your feet, and I will speak with you" (Ezek. 2:1); "Stand up; I am only a *mortal*" (Acts 10:26); "The voice of a god, and not of a *mortal*!" (Acts 12:22); "If I speak in the tongues of *mortals* and of angels, but do not have love . . ." (1 Cor. 13:1). This usage is much less frequent in the NIVI, though it still occurs: for example, "This is the voice of a god, not of a *mere mortal*" (Acts 12:22).

Dr. Grudem objects,

> This matters because the emphasis is different, for the word *mortal* shifts the emphasis from one's humanity to one's mortality (that is, one's liability to death). Peter [in Acts 10:26] does not refuse worship because he is "mortal" or one who is subject to death (in fact, he will live forever). He refuses worship because he is a creature made by God; he is not God, but

a man. . . . There is a perfectly good Greek adjective which means "mortal, subject to death" *(phthartos)*, but that is not the word Peter uses.[11]

I confess I rather dislike "mortal" in the vocative as God's term of address to Ezekiel: I find it slightly stilted. Nevertheless, I quickly confess that that reaction may just be my ears: someone else may not find it so. More important is the matter of semantics. My Webster's unabridged dictionary offers eleven listings under "mortal" *as an adjective,* and all of them are tied, directly or indirectly, to what Dr. Grudem calls "liability to death." Intriguingly, however, under the noun listing of "mortal," Webster's says, "man; a being subject to death; a human being." Semantically, then, the noun seems to be in the right ballpark, if Webster's has it right. On that ground I find it hard to object to using "mortal" as a noun in passages like Acts 10:26 and 12:22, whether or not it would be my own preferred rendering.

The Use of the Old Testament in the New

In chapter 1 (under "Some Historical Perspective"), I noted that 2 Samuel 7:14, with its singular "son" (referring in the first instance to Solomon), is quoted by the apostle Paul in 2 Corinthians 6:18 with the plural "sons and daughters." Already that warns us that in the case of Old Testament texts cited in the New, we should be careful about insisting on an exactitude of form that actually masks meaning or on a precision of form in which the apostle himself has little interest. One cannot fail to note, as well, that New Testament writers citing the Old Testament frequently change person: for example,

Exodus 13:2 (second person) = Luke 2:23 (third person)
1 Samuel 13:14 (third person) = Acts 13:22 (first person)
Psalm 68:18 (second person) = Ephesians 4:8 (third person)
Psalm 97:7 (second person) = Hebrews 1:6 (third person)

Isaiah 28:11 (third person) = 1 Corinthians 14:21 (first person)

These points make one hesitate before accepting CS principles A.1 and A.2.

But that is only one side of the matter. The other side is that it is possible to lose an inner-canonical link by inattention to details. Here the issues are so complex I cannot agree with formulas offered to resolve this challenge. I shall briefly comment on four passages.

First, consider 2 Samuel 7:14, referred to above—not only in its use in 2 Corinthians 6:18 (as above), but in the broader stream of "son" language in the Old Testament. As early as Exodus 4:22, Israel is called God's "son." Here in 2 Samuel 7:14, the king in the Davidic line is God's "son," and his appointment as king, his enthronement, is the moment when he becomes God's son, the moment when he is "begotten" (Psalm 2). Thus the king becomes the son *par excellence* among the people who are also called the "son" (see also Hosea 11:1). But eventually in the Old Testament there is rising hope for a "son" in the Davidic line who will properly and thoroughly mirror his "Father." That is precisely how the prophecy of Isaiah 9 is cast: to us a child is born, to us a son is given who will not only "reign on David's throne and over his kingdom," but who will also be called "the Mighty God, Everlasting Father" (9:6–7).

In other words, the "son" language at some point in the stream of redemptive history becomes overtly typological. Doubtless in God's mind it was always thus: in Exodus 4:22, we must suppose, God knew where the "son" language would ultimately wind up, and he begins by preparing the way with a growing pattern of biblical texts that finally explode in pregnant contexts that announce the coming of the "son"-messiah. There is intentionality in all of this—not merely a pattern into which Jesus conveniently fits but a divine intention to create a growing pattern that Jesus actually fulfills. It is important not to skew or mask such typologies.

Second, we must ask if a passage such as Psalm 34:19–20 fits into this pattern: "A righteous man may have many troubles, but the LORD delivers him from them all; he protects all his bones, not one of them will be broken" (NIV). The latter part is cited in John 19:36 with reference to Jesus at the time of his crucifixion: he was speared in the side rather than having his legs broken, and this was to fulfill this text from Psalm 34. Does not then the plural of the NIVI obscure the connection? "The righteous may have many troubles, but the LORD delivers them from them all; he protects all their bones, not one of them will be broken."

The thrust of the psalm at this juncture concerns righteous people in general (for example, Ps. 34:15ff.): note the plurals in 34:15–18: "The eyes of the LORD are on the righteous, and his ears are attentive to *their cry*. . . . The righteous cry out [plural], and the Lord hears *them*." True, verses 19–20 revert to the singular (a not uncommon phenomenon in the Psalms, as we have seen). Yet in all fairness this is likely a collective singular, for the psalm ends, "The LORD redeems his servants [plural]; no one will be condemned who takes refuge in him." In this instance, then, the ground upon which Jesus fulfills Psalm 34:19–20 is bound up with his being the archetypical righteous person. It is unclear to me that either Psalm 34 or John 19 demands that we hunt for some more teleological linkage.[12]

I do not understand why the plural "their bones" in Psalm 34:20 NIVI "makes the New Testament messianic use of the Psalm problematic."[13] It would be so *only* if every fulfillment quotation in the New Testament is related to the Old Testament source in one specific way, namely, as predictive utterance with univocal referent that is fulfilled in an explicit and exclusive event. Not for a moment do I deny that there are prophecies like that. But there are also types (of various kinds), examples, and an array of other kinds of connections.

Third, things are quite different in Psalm 69. This psalm, like Psalm 34, claims to be written by David. But much more of this psalm is written in the first-person singular. Several passages from this psalm are implicitly or explicitly said to be fulfilled in events in Jesus' life (Ps. 69:8, compare John 7:5; Ps. 69:9, compare John 2:17, Rom. 15:3; Ps. 69:21, compare Matt. 27:48, Mark 15:36, Luke 23:36) or in the early church (Ps. 69:25, compare Matt. 23:38, Acts 1:20). In some of these instances there is greater precision on very specific details.

I would want to argue that in these instances a tightly controlled typology is operating. The implicit argument is something like this: Granted that David is the paradigmatic king, the son of God, how much more shall what he suffered be fulfilled in the ultimate king, great David's greater son? Indeed, this line of thought ties in with the "suffering servant" motif in the New Testament. I would not want to lose such connections. Mercifully, in this case because the psalm was written in the first-person singular, which in English is not marked for gender, the singular has been preserved in our English translations (for example, both the NIV and NIVI), so there is no problem. But the challenge of handling typology responsibly is sometimes difficult. Great attention must be paid to the multitude of factors that properly contribute to the best translation.

Fourth, consider Psalm 8:4–6 and its use in Hebrews 2:6–8. I shall first set out the texts in the NIV and NIVI:

Psalm 8:4–6

NIV: "what *is man* that you are mindful of *him, the son of man* that you care for *him*? You made *him* a little lower than the heavenly beings and crowned *him* with glory and honor. You made *him* ruler over the works of your hands; you put everything under *his* feet."

NIVI: "what *are mere mortals* that you are mindful of *them, human beings* that you care for *them*?[14] You made *them* a little lower than the heavenly beings and crowned *them* with glory and honour. You made *them* rulers over the works of your hands; you put everything under *their* feet."

Hebrews 2:6–8

NIV: "But there is a place where someone has testified: 'What is *man* that you are mindful of him, the son of man that you care for him? You made him a little lower than the angels; you crowned him with glory and honor and put everything under his feet.' In putting everything under him, God left nothing that is not subject to him. Yet at present we do not see everything subject to him."

NIVI: "But there is a place where someone has testified: 'What is *a human being* that you are mindful of him, the son of man that you care for him? You made him a little lower than the angels; you crowned him with glory and honour and put everything under his feet.'[15] In putting everything under him, God left nothing that is not subject to him. Yet at present we do not see everything subject to him."

The NIVI more or less exchanges text and footnote in the Hebrews 2:6–8 passage.

Dr. Piper asserts, "The muting of masculinity in Psalm 8 is not preserved in Hebrews 2 when the Psalm is quoted, because it is evident that the writer of Hebrews sees messianic meaning in the wording of the Psalm."[16] I shall make several observations about these two passages and Dr. Piper's assertion:

1. These passages bring together several of the translation issues we have already dealt with: the meaning of "man" and "son of man," how to handle personal pronouns, the suitability of the rendering "mortals," and the various ways the New Testament cites the Old.

2. When Dr. Piper says that the NIVI of Psalm 8 mutes masculinity, once again he is conceding more than he may wish.

He is implying that "man" and "son of man" in his view *do* carry at least overtones of masculinity. But that is precisely why the CBT and others are pushing for gender-neutral translations: if people think that "man" carries masculine overtones even in a passage like Psalm 8, where the focus is on human beings as such or conceivably the human race as such, then it is time to abandon "man" in such contexts.

3. On the other hand, the CBT does not seem to have got its act together very well. Here Dr. Piper has a point. One could make a case for the NIVI text of Psalm 8 and the NIVI footnote of Hebrews 2, or one could make a case for the NIVI footnote of Psalm 8 and the NIVI text of Hebrews 2, but the actual combination strikes the reader as rather strange. After making all reasonable allowances for the difficulty of handling some Old Testament texts that are cited in the New, one does not expect translators to introduce unnecessary problems. Still, it is encouraging to observe how the CBT scholars were prepared to put aside their commitment to inclusive language when they were convinced that certain technical categories (above all, "son of man") were at stake.

4. Yet some of the criticisms that have been advanced against inclusive-language renderings of Psalm 8 in Hebrews 2 have been, in my view, a tad unfair. The commentaries are divided on the point I am about to raise, but the majority of the major commentaries adopt this stance, and I am persuaded they are right—even though I could justify this view only by a lengthy exegesis for which there is neither time nor space here. Hebrews 2 (they argue) does *not* present Jesus as the "son of man" in some technical, messianic sense. Rather, it presents Jesus as a human being, a true human being. He did not become an angel (2:5, 16—and no redeemer has arisen for fallen angels). Jesus had to belong to the same "family" as those he came to redeem (2:11); he had to become their brother (2:12). Since they have flesh and blood, that is, since they are human, he too shared in their humanity (2:14). This is the first necessary ingredient to his serving as a faithful

high priest for them (2:17). The author of Hebrews has already pointed out that along some axes human beings are "higher" than angels, for angels are "ministering spirits sent to serve those who will inherit salvation" (1:14). After all, the world to come has been assigned not to angels, but to human beings: God has put everything under their feet: that is the point of the quotation from Psalm 8 (Heb. 2:5–8). The trouble, of course, is that we do not yet see everything under the feet of human beings. But what do we see? We see Jesus (2:9). He became one with us humans, and thereby brings many "sons" (NIV; "sons and daughters," NIVI—an entirely reasonable rendering) to glory.

Thus if I understand the flow of Hebrews 2 aright, Psalm 8 is not a "messianic" psalm in the sense that, say, Psalm 110 is a messianic psalm. I still want the gender-related decisions made in one of these two passages to prevail in the other as well, but I am not convinced that those critics are right who say that terrible damage has been done by inclusive-language translations of this passage because they have somehow squeezed Christ to the periphery.

9

BUT IS THE ENGLISH LANGUAGE CHANGING?

The Debate

The question that is the title of this chapter raises the issue that lies behind so much of the rest of the debate. If spoken and written English have not changed, or have changed very little, then why this push to change translations that have served so long and well? In that case, of course, since the push must be coming from somewhere, and if (on this reading) it is not coming from changes in the language, it must be coming from feminists who are in charge of publishing houses that are pushing inclusive-language conformity down our throats. On the other hand, if the language is changing, then two options are possible. We may update our translations to accommodate the changes so that our Bibles will not be linguistically out of date. Alternatively, we may ascribe whatever gender changes that are developing in the language to feminist influence and then heartily oppose them.

The latter course is being pursued by the critics of gender-inclusive translations. At the risk of caricature (in which on

183

this issue I really do not wish to indulge), their argument runs something like this: (1) The English language is not changing, or not changing much. (2) If it is changing, we should oppose the changes because the feminists are behind the changes.

Several essays and short articles have been put forward along these lines. The nub of the argument is nicely summarized by Dr. Grudem.[1] He begins with about two and a half pages of examples of generic "he" and related pronouns, all drawn from recent newspapers *(Chicago Tribune, USA Today)*, magazines (Crain's *New York Business, Reader's Digest*), TV news programs *(Nightline)*, and the like, plus various authoritative sources on correct grammar. For example, "every college professor doesn't need to put *his* main energy into expanding the frontiers of knowledge" (*U.S. News and World Report*, December 30, 1996, 45–47). Then a slightly shorter section (a page and a half) treats the word "man" more or less the same way. For example, "Clean air and ozone obey no *manmade* boundaries" (*Chicago Tribune*, May 12, 1997, p. 1 headline).

In all fairness, however, some see things differently. Thus in a letter to the editor, Professor D. F. Wright, an evangelical historian at the University of Edinburgh, writes:

> Few human tasks can be as important as translating the Bible from its original languages into contemporary vernacular languages.
>
>   It is therefore remarkable, indeed almost shocking, that sweeping guidelines on one of the most sensitive demands of the translators' task should emerge from a single meeting at Colorado Springs. . . . This surely must be said, regardless of the details of the agreed guidelines. In the event, one should not be surprised to find them seriously inadequate.
>
>   I have not seen the inclusive-language version NIV, and hold no brief for it. But I am dismayed that the over-reaction to it in Colorado Springs evinced so little sensitivity to the cultural and social changes that have brought about significant linguistic shifts in common English. It simply will not

do to target "secular feminism" alone. To ignore these shifts, Canute-like, will reinforce the tendency of some evangelical communities to dwell in cultural ghettos. For many others, it will shorten the shelf-life of the NIV. Numerous Bible-believing evangelicals now find the traditional use of "man" and "men" in contexts where male(s) are not indicated variously grating, embarrassing and inconsiderate, both to my fellow-Christians and to those outsiders who thereby have a non-gospel stumbling block placed in their path towards faith.[2]

So which side has the truth of the matter?

Some Reflections

History of the Issue

The issue is not entirely new. One of the best summaries of earlier discussion is found in the work of Baron.[3] In 1770 Robert Baker recommended the construction "one . . . one's" rather than "one . . . his" if not balanced by "one . . . hers." This has been picked up repeatedly: for example, "Every man and woman is the architect of one's own fortune" (Wolstan Dixey, 1884). A century later, Lillian E. Carlton (1979) recommends "As anybody can see for one's self."

In the same way, singular "they" has a long history, stretching back to the sixteenth century, and including such prestigious writers as Addison, Austen, Fielding, Chesterfield, Ruskin, and Scott. Indeed, some authorities argue that this option was more common before 1850 or so, when grammarians became a little more purist on the matter of formal agreement and therefore insisted on generic "he." There is also a strong tradition that uses the plural pronoun in the singular: not only the first-person plural "we" for "I" (which can be traced back to Old English), but at some point during the fourteenth century "you," originally restricted to the plural, supplanted the second-person singular "thou" in some circles, even though it took quite a while to win the entire populace.

Baron notes that some grammarians "approve of the singular *they*."[4] These include Alexander Bain, *A Higher English Grammar* (1879); Henry Sweet, *A New English Grammar* (1891, 1931); Otto Jespersen, *A Modern English Grammar on Historical Principles* (1922, citing many examples); George Curme, *A Grammar of the English Language* (1931); and Randolph Quirk, *A Grammar of Contemporary English* (1972). On the other hand, resistance to singular "they" appears in the eighteenth century and gains strength into the nineteenth. By the early twentieth century, H. W. Fowler (1926) admits that singular "they" is popular in British usage, but he insists that the construction "anybody can see for themselves," although popular, "sets the literary man's teeth on edge." Edward D. Johnson (1982) takes much the same line.

The problem of the gender-marked English personal pronoun has thus been discussed for a long time. Some who defend generic "he" and related pronouns have nevertheless conceded that this solution is not ideal: so, for instance, H. W. Fowler and F. G. Fowler in *The King's English* (1906). But at the popular level "they" has held its own for centuries, and it is now in resurgence. Some authorities now support it: for example, the lexicographer Alma Graham (1973). Certainly the various attempts to *create* an alternative pronoun—more than eighty attempts, including such blendings as *thon, he'er, shem*—have all sunk without a trace. Nevertheless, some anomalies not only persist but are universally acknowledged. "Everyone liked the dinner but he did not care for the dessert" is, as Baron acknowledges, "impossible English; only the plural personal pronouns will do in such a case."[5]

What are we to make of this? Critics of gender-inclusive language might well conclude that on the long haul, it looks as if we are stuck with "he," so we might as well make the most of it. My point is simpler. Although I would not want to minimize the influence of various feminist lobbies on English usage, the underlying pressures for change have been there for centuries.[6] We should therefore be exceedingly careful about monocausational analyses of the changes taking place, with simple wrong-versus-right prescriptions.

Causes of Language Change

For reasons still to be advanced, I am persuaded that in the Western English-speaking countries we are undergoing changes in the area of grammatical gender that are deep, fairly widespread, and probably not reversible. What has brought them about? Here I shall mention two factors, apart from the tensions in the language already present and straining for relief. Doubtless there are others.

First, there is no downplaying the importance of feminist influence. Nevertheless, I would argue:

a. Regardless of the source of the pressure for linguistic change, it is important to recognize that alternative grammatical gender systems are not intrinsically evil. That was one of the purposes of including chapter 4. The substance of Scripture can be conveyed in *any* language, and that is being done all the time, even in languages with gender systems far, far removed from those with which we are familiar in the Indo-European family. Of course, no translation is perfect: "translation is treason." But granted the sheer diversity of gender systems in languages around the world, and that many of these systems change slowly with time, it betrays a serious ignorance of language structures, including gender systems, and of the nature of translation, when a shift in the system of a receptor language is tagged with evil epithets, or the resulting translations are judged mistranslations. I have tried to show that what the original sources actually say can always be got across in the receptor language, even if not the same way, and even if some explanatory note is required, and even if in particular constructions one may sometimes provide a for-

mal equivalent to one element in a construction but not
to another, and so forth.

b. Regardless of the source of the pressure for linguistic
change, the changes (I shall argue) are here. If that is
the case, *this is the language that, increasingly, we have
to work with,* even if we may not approve all the reasons that have brought these changes about (even as
some did not appreciate the reasons for dropping "thou"
and "thy"). In short, whatever the reasons for the
changes in the English language now taking place, the
translator's job is always the same: translate the Word
of God into the *current* language.

c. In wishing to preserve what we understand God to be
saying about the relationships between men and women
in the home and church, we who are complementarians
will often prove more convincing if we frankly acknowledge the degree to which ungodly sexism *has* hurt
women. Every pastor has had to deal with battered
wives. Surely no Christian with a concern for justice
wishes to support unequal pay for equal work performed
by people with equal experience and competence. In
short, I worry about "putting a fence around Torah."
Eventually Torah itself is no longer heard. I worry about
the swing of the pendulum. Because in my view egalitarians and other feminists interpret certain Scriptures
poorly and succumb to current pressures, this does not
justify a cultural swing to the "right" that fails to deal
firmly with genuine injustice. So also with respect to
the changes taking place in the English language. I see
little reason to fight a modification in the gender system
of the English language, since as far as I can see I can
convey the truth of Scripture regardless of gender system (even if in different ways); I can see many reasons
for helping the oppressed on the one hand and for insisting on biblical structures and role relationships on the

other. Those things are mandated regardless of whether I am working in Hebrew, English, Qafar, or Kikuyu.

Second, we cannot deny, I think, that some of the pressure for change springs from a profound abandonment of the Bible's worldview, the Bible's culture, the Bible's story line, as that has been mediated to us by various English Bibles.[7] I mourn the loss. But on the long haul, we cannot change this trend by merely defensive postures that legislate *against* things. Sooner or later, we will fall under judgment, or by the grace of God we will reverse trends by the powerful proclamation of the life-transforming, culture-changing gospel.

Generic "He"

As for the evidence adduced that English still uses "he" and related pronouns in a generic sense, I must say two things.

First, the third-person singular pronoun is by far the most difficult thing to handle for those who wish to write gender-inclusive English. It is therefore unsurprising that there are still many, many examples around of the unreconstructed generic "he." No one is arguing that the change has been universal.

Second, to quote examples like this, all on one side, does not fairly assess how far the changes have gone. What other authorities are there? More important, how many of these same sources alternate between gender-neutral language and more traditional language? For many publications the changes are not fixed. Further, some use "he" generically and then a few pages on use "she" generically. Above all, what is the balance of gender-neutral usage in current English as compared with, say, thirty years ago? I know of no study that has tried to probe this carefully, but I would be surprised if such a study did not reveal a very substantial shift indeed.

Since starting to write this manuscript three or four weeks ago, I have read several books on the side. It dawned on me to start checking. Without exception, examples of gender-neutral language were not hard to find. I found consistent care taken in this respect by Carl Sagan in his last book, *Billions and Billions*.[8] Ah, you say, what do you expect? Carl Sagan could not be accused of having conservative sympathies. But I also read Terry Eagleton, *The Illusions of Postmodernism*.[9] He is not, of course, a Christian writer. He is a well-informed socialist. Nevertheless, this book is "reactionary" against the powerful trends toward postmodern thought in our culture. After using "he" in a generic sense on several occasions, Eagleton is capable of writing a sentence such as this: "First of all, socialism, which like widespread virtue is only feasible if you are reasonably well-heeled as a society, would considerably augment the primary goods available to each individual for her pursuit of happiness, by seeking to eliminate want."[10] Still, you say, that is not distinctively *Christian* writing. Too true. But I also read the award-winning book by Cornelius Plantinga Jr., *Not the Way It's Supposed to Be: A Breviary of Sin*.[11] There I found a book without a trace of the more traditional gender system. Even when "he" is used generically (as it sometimes is), one finds counterbalancing clauses such as "this child may take her vengeance thirty years later."[12] Then to top it off, on the way home I turned on the radio in the car and learned from CBS news that Voyager I is now "humankind's farthest object in space."[13] Eventually I arrived home, and after supper reached for the latest *Time* magazine. Within a minute my eyes fell on the sentence, "If the conspirators get their way, will the next President have to sign an affidavit about whom he or she has ever slept with?"[14]

In short, anyone can make up her own list. But the changes are farther advanced in the English language than the critics think, even if not as far advanced as some feminists think. When a language is right in the middle of a major transition, that is when the most virulent disputes will break out as to how to proceed in a translation. Older readers of this little book will remember how heated some discussions were fifty years ago, in some conservative circles, over "thee" and "thou."

Varieties of English

We have to face the fact that even within America or Great Britain there are, at certain levels of analysis, many "Englishes." This is more than a matter of pronunciation. It includes idiom, vocabulary, and the degree to which a region is on the "front edge" of change or on the "back edge" of change. That affects all of us, myself included. I am influenced by the fact that I have spent a fair bit of time during the past decade taking my turn in university missions and the like. I do not want the old NIV when I am expounding the earlier chapters of, say, Romans in an evangelistic setting in a university. Nothing is gained by it, and too much is lost. I'd much rather use the NIVI. But doubtless I think this way, at least in part, because university missions form part of *my* constituency. Yet I acknowledge that concerns about gender-neutral language are more common in universities than in blue-collar factories, more common in the New England states and in the Pacific Northwest than in the Bible belt, and so forth. And likewise, the critics of the NIVI have their subcultures and constituencies as well.

When we extend these parameters to wherever English is spoken worldwide, the analysis of trends is even more difficult, for English is the second or third language, or the language of education, of huge swaths of the world's population. I think I have a pretty good feel for what is happening to the English language in half a dozen countries, but I have very little idea about what is happening to it in, say, Nigeria.

We thus return by another route to a discussion I began earlier in the book. Whether we like it or not, now that the KJV no longer dominates the Protestant world, various English translations have constituencies. The desire of the CBT and the copyright holder to keep the NIV up-to-date by incremental changes was a good one for all kinds of reasons. The nature of incremental changes entails the policy that only the latest edition is kept in print. But the vast share of the evangelical market occupied by the NIV doubtless ensures that anything more than incidental changes would eventually stir up at least some negative reaction, and in this case something still more furious. Whether changes to the NIV are possible in the future I cannot say. But if not, sooner or later it will fade in its popularity, displaced by some other version. It may be that something like the NIVI will be produced under its own name in due course and find its own constituency. I wish Bibles did not have constituencies; I wish there were one English Bible used everywhere. But that day is past. The fact is that this wishful thinking cannot be imposed. Moreover, with the extraordinary variations now operative in worldwide English, perhaps constituency Bibles, even if inevitable, are in part a good thing.

For exactly these reasons, arguments about what "sounds" right turn out to be remarkably subjective. Ten years ago many of the instances of "humankind" or "human beings" or generic "her" I found in contemporary literature struck me as strange. Now I rarely notice them; I have to look for them to spot such occurrences. If all of them strike you as strange, that says as much about what you have been reading (or not reading) as anything. Of course, this does not mean that no expression should ever be condemned as cumbersome or inept. It does mean that this weapon of labeling should be used with some restraint, for linguistic fads sometimes change public perception on such points remarkably quickly.

Inclusive language has not swept everything in front of it away. As I am not a prophet, I cannot predict what the next step will be. A deep reactionary movement is not impossible. Yet so far as I can see, the move toward inclusive language in the English-speaking world has not yet come close to cresting. Doubtless all kinds of inconsistencies and traditional forms of expression will remain, perhaps for a long time, perhaps indefinitely. But as far as I can read the situation, the times they are a-changing—and the English language with them.

10

PASTORAL CONSIDERATIONS

HOW TO AVOID BIBLE RAGE

Suffer a word of admonition—a half dozen of them, in fact.

1. Let us aim to raise standards of journalistic integrity. By "us," I mean Christians. *World* bills itself as a weekly news magazine like *Time,* except that readers can believe what it prints. Do you want readers to believe you simply because you adopt "conservative" positions on most issues? In that case, you will convince the convinced. But if you wish to convince others who are not (yet) in your camp, your journalistic standards must be beyond reproach.

On all kinds of issues I badly want the voice of *World* to be heard. But frankly, I have many friends to whom I would never recommend *World,* precisely because, as in the case of the original article by Susan Olasky, the tenor is grating, the research shoddy, the argument a long way from being even-handed, and the focus obscure. In an essay allegedly on Bible translations, complete with an attention-grabbing cover that impugned the motives of all those with whom *World* disagrees on this issue, the article displayed no grasp at all of the most basic elements of linguistics and translation. Ms. Olasky referred to precisely three Bible texts and then devoted far more space to Willow Creek and women's ordination than to Bible translations (thereby linking the two topics irrefragably, when in the minds of many, many people, including complementarians, the two issues, though related, are separable). Yet the article managed to get a good man fired from his seminary and incite enough hate that destroyed Bibles were mailed to IBS headquarters.

Some of *World*'s later treatments of the matter, though I disagreed with them, included more substance and at least a show of evenhandedness, and I am grateful. But instead of insisting that they did nothing wrong, it would be a great help in this fray if the publisher and Susan Olasky published an apology for that first piece—unless, of course, they believe that the end justifies the means.

Let me address *World* directly. I'm not asking you to change your editorial opinion. Just swallow some humble pie on this one and resolve to be more careful and much kinder on the next issue, without sacrificing journalistic punch. Apply the Golden Rule to the way you treat your opponents: would you not want them to treat you fairly, even when they disagree with you? Your credibility will go up, and I for one will be able to start recommending you to friends.

2. On complex issues, let us slow down. I know that some issues demand urgent action, or it will be too late. But inclusive-language Bible translations have been around for about a decade. Suddenly everything has to be resolved in a matter of weeks. Enduring and binding guidelines are hammered out in a hotel room overnight. We bang the drum to get a lot of people to sign these guidelines. But these principles are profoundly flawed, even when they are saying some important things. The guidelines of the CBT, worked out by many com-

petent people over a long period of time, also have some flaws. Not for a moment am I suggesting I have all the answers. But I do think I have demonstrated that these matters are complex, and on the long haul we will do less damage to our credibility and prove more helpful to the church of Jesus Christ if we discern when issues are sufficiently complex that it is the part of wisdom to go slowly and softly and to consult with others with demonstrable expertise in the area.

3. Let us avoid impugning the motives of the other side. Of course, there are people of integrity on both sides of this issue, and I am grateful. But I found articles that lambasted Zondervan for its money-grubbing greed. The only reason Zondervan wants to put out an inclusive-language translation is so that they can make a lot of money, they said; imagine—controlling and domesticating translation policy of God's most holy Word so as to make money.

Of course, this line of argument plays well with certain kinds of troops. But quite apart from its meanness, we might reflect that *(a)* if Zondervan is going to make a lot of money by inclusive-language translations, then the English language has changed a lot more than the critics admit that it has; *(b)* the way that some of the critics forced Zondervan to back off its publishing plans was by denominational threats, in effect, to withhold money; and *(c)* conservative organs, including *World,* doubtless enjoyed a boost in circulation out of this as well.

4. Let us try to avoid entrenched positions that demonize the other side. I have recently read again all the *World* articles on this subject, and the scholars who make up the CBT, as these articles present them, are pretty horrible people. I do not personally know all the members of the CBT, but I know quite a few of them. Some of them are among the godliest, most competent, experienced, mature Christian thinkers and scholars I know—and not a few of them are complementarians to boot. Each side needs to try harder to avoid demonizing the other side. I know the convictions on the issues are deeply held. But on the long haul, are we more interested in winning

brothers and sisters to the truth as we understand it or in scoring points with our own constituencies?

We all fall into these traps, of course. But one of the things I liked about the late Francis Schaeffer is that even when he was uttering strong denunciations, he usually managed to do it with compassion. John Newton says it best:

> Zeal is that pure and heavenly flame
>   The fire of love supplies;
> While that which often bears the name
>   Is self in a disguise.
>
> True zeal is merciful and mild,
>   Can pity and forbear;
> The false is headstrong, fierce and wild,
>   And breathes revenge and war.
>
> While zeal for truth the Christian warms,
>   He knows the worth of peace;
> But self contends for names and forms,
>   Its party to increase.

5. Let us try to avoid manipulative language. If I include samples here, I shall lose friends on both sides of this issue, and in any case I have no desire to be unkind. In the heat of debate, we all slip sometimes. But arguments that tie your opinion to Christian orthodoxy in such a way that believers who are no less orthodox but who read the evidence another way have the effect of marginalizing and manipulating people who, in your best moments, you yourself would happily acknowledge to be orthodox. Avoid arguments like that. And note the irony: the most manipulative arguments in some of these kinds of debate are the "spiritual" ones.

6. Let us be careful what we sign on to. At a guess, quite a few of those who signed the CSG did so because they felt strongly about issues surrounding complementarianism and

egalitarianism, not because they claimed to know much about linguistic theory and translation theory. But that is another way of warning one another that *especially* when we hold strong theological convictions in some area, we need to be careful about transferring those convictions to adjacent or related areas where closer inspection may inform us that the ties are not as close as first appeared to be the case.

I have heard more than a few critics insist that there must be at least some measure of conspiracy going on, since some of the CBT members are egalitarians, and the preface to the NIVI does say some pretty sloppy things. That may be; I cannot tell. But equally, it is difficult for defenders of inclusive language not to conclude that at least some of their critics are far more motivated by a certain social agenda regarding men and women, which the critics believe to be biblical, than by an evenhanded and competent desire to get translations right. That may be; I cannot tell. But we ought to strive with extra diligence to be evenhanded precisely in those areas where we feel most strongly about matters.

NOTES

Preface

1. "Egalitarians" believe that the Bible teaches that men and women are so equal that no distinctions in role should be maintained—whether in home or church or elsewhere—that are grounded in their respective genders. "Complementarians" hold that the Bible teaches equality of importance and significance (for both are made in the image of God), but that distinctions are made that assign complementary roles in home and church.

Chapter 1: *The Making of a Crisis: Bible Translation and Bible Rage*

1. Bruce Manning Metzger, *Reminiscences of an Octogenarian* (Peabody, Mass.: Hendrickson, 1997), 79. Of course, this judgment is specific to the West: even during the past few years, a handful of Bible translators working in so-called third-world countries have paid with their lives for the privilege of translating the Word of God.

2. See the report in *Christianity Today* 41.8 (July 14, 1997), 62.

3. These figures can easily be verified with the appropriate Bible software, but it was John Kohlenberger III who brought them to my attention. See John R. Kohlenberger III, "Understanding the Current Controversy over Bible Translations" (paper presented at the international convention of the Christian Booksellers Association, Atlanta, Ga., July 14, 1997). A slightly edited version of this paper is available online at http://www.worldstar.com/~jrk3/inclusive.htm.

4. Or owing simply to the *perception* of shifts in English usage: the result is the same. As I have said, I shall return to the question of how much English actually is changing in chapter 9. I cannot keep alluding to that chapter, and it would become tedious to qualify every mention of shifts in the language by adding an additional "or perception of shifts" or the like. I shall make occasional reference to this debate before chapter 9, but I beg the reader's indulgence on this point for the time being.

5. I have provided concrete figures comparing the sales of these two Bibles and several others in "New Bible Translations: An Assessment and Prospect," in *The Bible in the Twenty-First Century,* ed. Howard Clark Kee (Philadelphia: Trinity Press International, 1993), 61–63.

6. From the preface to the CEV, titled "Welcome to the Contemporary English Version" (emphasis original).

7. From the preface to the NRSV, titled "To the Reader."

8. With two others, I reviewed the NRSV when it was first presented to the Society of Biblical Literature. The review was subsequently published as "A Review of the New Revised Standard Version," *Reformed Theological Review* 50 (1991): 1–11.

9. I set these out in chapter 2.

10. To make this point clearer, one might introduce traditional Tonga culture. There the practice of kissing is inappropriate between adults of either sex. It is a suitable sign of affection only between a mother and her baby. The mention of the "mouth" in the context of "kissing" is vulgar. Thus a passage such as "O that you would kiss me with the kisses of your mouth! For your love is better than wine . . ." (Song of Sol. 1:2 RSV) would be understood by the average Tonga reader to be an utterance by a notorious prostitute. See Ernst R. Wendland, *The Cultural Factor in Bible Translation,* UBS Monograph Series 2 (London: United Bible Societies, 1987), 1–2.

11. *World* 12.2 (March 29, 1997), 12–15.

12. Ibid., 12.

13. Ibid.

14. *World* 12.5 (April 19, 1997), 16.

15. For example, "Think about it. NIV translators knuckle under to a British partner whose concern is neither accuracy nor truth, but money! And this comes out of England, which since Spurgeon's death has basked in its liberalism and has become so deficient in its evangelistic efforts as to lose its own nation. . . . What will be next at Willow Creek—openness to same-sex marriages, even more openness to the killing of preborns in the wombs of their mothers?" (*National Liberty Journal* 26.5 [May 1997], 22).

16. Dr. Barker and Dr. Youngblood went to Colorado Springs not as duly appointed representatives of the CBT, but only as informed individuals.

17. Wheaton, Ill.: Crossway, 1991.

18. The May 31/June 7 edition of *World* reported the earlier developments and offered a brief critique of one element of the translation principles of the Committee on Bible Translation, but was apparently unable to include the events of May 27 in its pages.

19. I should acknowledge that I was one of those who resigned. Perhaps I should add that ، also disagree with some of the principles adopted by the CBT.

20. *World* (12.22 [October 18, 1997], 19) promptly branded this group the opposition. But anyone who has talked at length with representatives from these groups knows that technical questions about translation principles dealing with gender language are emerging from complementarians among them no less than from egalitarians.

21. In deference to their convictions, I use this term in its generic sense; there are three women in this list of names: Vonette Bright, Mary Kassian, and Dorothy Patterson.

22. *Christianity Today* 41.12 (October 27, 1997), 14–15.

Chapter 2: Conflicting Principles: The CBT and CSG on Inclusive Language

1. *CBMW News* 2.4 (September 1997), 9.

2. Adopted August 1992.

3. The copy of the CBT policy I was sent includes at this point a parenthetical "Note," in small print, as follows: "This 'principle' articulates a *basic* principle of translation actually followed by CBT in its work on the NIV but not stated in the original 'Translators' Manual' adopted in 1968 (enclosed). It had in view the use of euphemisms in translation such as 'one male' in place of the Hebrew expression 'one who urinates against a wall' (for example, 1 Sam. 25:22) or 'genitals' for Hebrew 'flesh,' a Hebrew euphemism for penis (for example, Ezek. 23:20)."

4. I am providing the latest form available to me, but I will indicate in the notes the changes from the initially agreed on draft.

5. The original added "or human beings in general" after "the human race." The additional words were deleted "because the phrase was confusing and widely misunderstood. Many people thought we meant that women should always be called 'men,' which we surely did not intend!" (*CBMW News* 2.4 [September 1997], 9).

6. All the words from "however" to the end have been added in this revision, owing to some further research in Greek lexica and literature.

7. The words from "and that some" to the end are added in this revision. The CBMW explanation (*CBMW News* 2.4 [September 1997], 9) says that the endorsers "recognize that there may yet be new information or more precise ways of formulating certain things, but they would only be refinements, not fundamental changes."

Chapter 3: Translation and Treason: An Inevitable and Impossible Task

1. The "or all" hints at a major dispute among Greek specialists wrestling with a branch of linguistics called aspect theory, as it is applied to Hellenistic Greek.

2. This example is also developed by John R. Kohlenberger III, "Understanding the Current Controversy over Bible Translations" (paper presented at the international convention of the Christian Booksellers Association,

Atlanta, Ga., July 14, 1997); available online at http://www.worldstar
.com/~jrk3/ inclusive.htm.

3. John Beekman and John Callow, *Translating the Word of God* (Grand
Rapids: Zondervan, 1974), 29.

4. *Mark Twain: Collected Tales, Sketches, Speeches, and Essays,
1852–1890,* ed. Louis J. Budd (New York: Library of America, 1992), 588.

5. Ibid.

6. Ibid., 589.

7. Ibid., 590.

8. Ibid., 598.

9. See Jan de Waard and Eugene A. Nida, *From One Language to
Another: Functional Equivalence in Bible Translating* (Nashville: Thomas
Nelson, 1986), 42: "There is always some loss in the communication
process, for sources and receptors never have identical linguistic and cultural backgrounds. . . . The translator's task, however, is to keep such loss
at a minimum."

10. By "absolute" I mean that these two words alone constitute the
clause under discussion. There are many other instances when *egō eimi* is
part of a larger expression that includes a complement, for example, "*I am*
the bread of life" (John 6:35), or an adverb, for example, "where *I am*"
(John 7:34—and here the two critical Greek words are in reverse order).

11. Strictly speaking, the NASB offers "I am *He*," because of its capi-
talization policy, the italics also indicating, as its footnote states, that the
text is literally "I am."

12. Compare John 4:26. The Samaritan woman has been talking about
the Messiah, and Jesus claims, "*Egō eimi ho lalōn soi.*" Formally, this could
be rendered, "I am the one speaking to you," with "the one speaking to you"
providing the complement. But that is so unbearably trite that almost everyone takes it to mean (still rendered pretty formally), "I am, the one speaking
to you"—that is, "the one speaking to you" is now in apposition to "I." But
that means, in this context, that the "I am" part most naturally reads as "I am
(the Christ)." In other words, the complement is established by the context.
Thus after the Samaritan woman's mention of the Christ, the NIV renders, "I
who speak to you am he [that is, the Christ]."

13. See Barry J. Beitzel, "Exodus 3:14 and the Divine Name: A Case
of Biblical Paronomasia," *Trinity Journal* 1 (1980): 5–20, which, despite
the title, examines many examples, not just one.

14. Quoted by F. F. Bruce, *History of the Bible in English: From the
Earliest Versions,* 3d ed. (New York: Oxford University Press, 1978),
19–20; cited also in Kohlenberger, "Understanding" (under the heading
"'Word-for-Word' vs. 'Phrase-for-Phrase'").

15. Robert Martin, *Accuracy of Translation* (Edinburgh: Banner of Truth
Trust, 1989), 29–31 and throughout.

16. See especially Ernst-August Gutt, *Translation and Relevance: Cog-
nition and Context* (Oxford: Blackwell, 1991).

17. It is possible to abuse what is in fact an elementary principle by imagining a narrow group of readers with a special focus. For example, the way Paul's language about homosexuality *functions* in Romans 1 among heterosexual Christian readers, who presumably approve of what he is saying, cannot be preserved, say, among contemporary English-speaking homosexual pagans. True enough, but this has nothing to do with translation: the same could be said for first-century Greek-speaking homosexual pagans. No translator who wrestles with the performative aspects of language or with speech act theory wants to wrench such matters to the fore and sacrifice other semantic components (that is, components of meaning). It is simply a matter of drawing attention to aspects of language that are often overlooked.

18. For example, Eugene A. Nida and Charles R. Taber, *The Theory and Practice of Translation,* Helps for Translators 8 (Leiden: E. J. Brill, 1974), 4: "Anything that can be said in one language can be said in another, unless the form is an essential part of the message."

19. As it develops, the NET Bible will become available in print, but it can also be viewed online at http://www.bible.org/netbible/index.htm. Obviously "NET" is a pun: it is an abbreviation of New English Translation, yet from the beginning the plan has been to make it available on the (Inter)net. I am grateful to Dr. W. Hall Harris III for showing me some of the page proofs.

20. The closest thing would be the kinds of interlinears where, say, Hebrew lines are interleaved with English renderings that try to convey the semantic contribution not only of each word but of each morpheme. The result is not a translation at all, of course, but a crib for Hebrew students.

21. The turning point was the book by de Waard and Nida, *From One Language to Another.* Another weakness in the initial definition of "dynamic equivalence" was that by focusing on the ability of the reader to comprehend and respond, it ignored what are in fact very considerable difficulties in some biblical texts. Recall the shrewd remark by Bishop Stephen Neill, "Translating the Word of God," *Churchman* 90 (1976): 287: "I remember once exploding angrily in the Tamil Bible translation committee, when we had so smoothed out the complex passage Galatians 2:1–10 as to conceal completely the tensions and confusions which underlie the apostle's twisted grammar. This we had no right to do."

22. The bibliography is now very substantial. The latest contribution by Ernst-August Gutt is "Implicit Information in Literary Translation: A Relevance-Theoretic Perspective," *Target* 8.2 (1996): 239–56.

23. I have tried to wrestle at some length with the theoretical issues in *The Gagging of God* (Grand Rapids: Zondervan, 1996).

24. As an aside, I should mention contemporary efforts to get around this blanket statement by computer translations. The translation programs are becoming remarkably sophisticated. The best of them now produce more or less readable results when they are translating material that is factual, scientific, technical, full of standard technical expressions, stereo-

typed—such as scientific papers. They are far less effective when it comes to well-crafted novels, special genres, creative writing, poetry, symbol-laden works, and so forth. As computers become more powerful they will be able to check results not only against the priorities of the translation program itself, but against larger and larger databases that provide appropriate and inappropriate matches. But (1) it is difficult to see how such programs will ever overcome all the problems when the text is not cast in standard, scientific terminology; (2) more important, the ways in which computers solve these problems are not open to human translators anyway: our minds cannot perform the massive sorts for matches essential to the procedures of computers.

25. A hybrid option is just barely possible. IBS and Zondervan could make incremental changes in the current NIV as long as such changes did not touch anything related to gender-inclusive language. That would be a kind of self-restricted option *c*. Realistically, that option, even if pursued for a while, cannot endure for more than an edition or two.

26. It must be admitted that some authors use "meaning" and "sense" in slightly different ways. The niceties need not detain us here. Compare Moisés Silva, *Biblical Words and Their Meaning*, rev. and expanded ed. (Grand Rapids: Zondervan, 1994), 101–18; and Arthur Gibson, *Biblical Semantic Logic: A Preliminary Analysis* (New York: St. Martin's Press, 1981), 47–59.

27. "Moses" sounds like a Hebrew word meaning "to draw out," "Abraham" like a Hebrew phrase meaning "father of a multitude."

Chapter 4: Gender and Sex around the World: A Translator's Nightmare

1. In this section I lean heavily on Greville G. Corbett, *Gender* (Cambridge: Cambridge University Press, 1991), a standard text; and to some extent on Dennis E. Baron, *Grammar and Gender* (New Haven: Yale University Press, 1986)—in addition, of course, to notes sent by Dr. Norman Fraser, to which I have already referred.

2. I keep saying "normally" and "generally" because many complex exceptions exist, usually with well-understood structures. For example, the Greek neuter plural subject may take a singular verb, but the Greek masculine or feminine plural subject must take a plural verb.

3. German nouns are always capitalized.

4. See Norman M. Fraser and Greville G. Corbett, "Gender, Animacy, and Declensional Class Assignment in Russian," in *Yearbook of Morphology 1994*, ed. Geert Booij and Jaap van Marle (Dordrecht: Kluwer, 1995), 123–50.

5. On this last point, see Corbett, *Gender*, 315.

6. More than eighty different forms have been proposed by those attempting to create such a pronoun in English.

7. That is, elements in a coordinate structure.

8. Briefly, see Corbett, *Gender*, 310–18.

9. What makes Chinese difficult for Westerners is not its syntax but (1) phonologically, its use of pitch; and (2) orthographically, its thousands of characters.

10. The two that follow I draw from Corbett (*Gender,* 321), though in fact they appear elsewhere as well.

11. Behind these observations is an array of far more complex issues that I cannot take the space to deal with here. This side of the Enlightenment, many linguists and cognitive scientists have thought of reason as disembodied, abstract, atomistic, extrinsic to any particular cultural expression. Under the impact of postmodern epistemology, another view is gradually establishing itself among linguists: thought is necessarily embodied in this or that language system, it is thus concrete, may be imaginative, and is inevitably tied to specific language structures (which are themselves, of course, part of particular cultural expression). See, for example, George Lakoff, *Women, Fire, and Dangerous Things: What Categories Reveal about the Mind* (Chicago: University of Chicago Press, 1987). In my view, the postmodern critique of virtually autonomous post-Enlightenment human reason is largely correct (though elsewhere I have criticized various facets of the postmodern enterprise: see my *Gagging of God* [Grand Rapids: Zondervan, 1996]). The entailment of the view well represented by Lakoff is a further strengthening of the position that no translation of extended text is ever mechanical. It always involves an interpretive element. One is not tapping into disembodied truth that has been captured in one language one way and in another language another way. Omniscience may see things that way, but finite language users cannot. Important as these issues are, they would take us too far afield if we were to probe them satisfactorily here.

12. I here borrow an example from Baron, *Grammar and Gender,* 195.

13. Rodney Venberg, "The Problem of a Female Deity in Translation," *Bible Translator* 22.2 (1971): 68–70.

14. Wayne Grudem, "What's Wrong with Gender-Neutral Bible Translations?" (Libertyville, Ill.: CBMW, 1997), 15. This is really a second edition of a circulated paper. Unless otherwise specified, this is the edition to which I refer.

15. Ibid., 9 (emphasis his).

Chapter 5: *A Brief Evaluation of the CBT and CS Principles*

1. Perhaps it should be said that the CBT principles were prepared for in-house use, that is, as guidelines to the committee as it switched over to inclusive-language translation. If the CBT guidelines had been intended for public consumption, doubtless more care would have been taken in their wording to avoid the possibility of misunderstanding.

2. Compare the intention of Bruce Metzger, with respect to the NRSV: he and the committee intended to eliminate "masculine-oriented language concerning people, so far as this could be done without distorting passages that reflect the historical situation of ancient patriarchal culture and soci-

ety" (*Reminiscences of an Octogenarian* [Peabody, Mass.: Hendrickson, 1997], 89).

3. Occasionally a simile drawn from motherhood is applied to God; he is never addressed as "Mother" in Scripture.

4. For example: "I strongly disagree with this procedure. The evangelical doctrine of Scripture is that every word of the original is exactly what God wanted it to be, because 'all Scripture is God-breathed' (2 Tim. 3:16). If God caused Psalm 1 to be written with singular nouns and pronouns, then we should reflect the sense of those words in English translation. We must not 'substitute' other words with different senses" (Wayne Grudem, "What's Wrong with Gender-Neutral Bible Translations?" [Libertyville, Ill.: CBMW, 1997], 11). That is exactly the argument used to defend the preservation of singular "thou" a few decades ago. The common problem is the failure to recognize that preserving God's words in Psalm 1 means preserving Hebrew words, which are tied to semantic ranges, syntactical structures, gender and number systems, morphology, and other phenomena that are radically different in English—and further that English is changing. This emotive way of putting things implies that those who disagree with Dr. Grudem's views on translation are disparaging or ignoring "the evangelical doctrine of Scripture." Most emphatically is that not the case, and it would be exceedingly helpful if the charge, doubtless made in good faith, were withdrawn.

5. This one I have culled from John R. Kohlenberger III, "Understanding the Current Controversy over Bible Translations" (paper presented at the international convention of the Christian Booksellers Association, Atlanta, Ga., July 14, 1997); available online at http://www.worldstar.com/~jrk3/inclusive.htm.

6. For example, the RSV (1952) still preserved the archaizing forms in direct address to God. These have disappeared in the NRSV.

7. As in all Scripture quotations in this book, italics signal emphases that I have inserted to draw attention to some linguistic phenomenon in the text.

8. Mark L. Strauss, "Linguistic and Hermeneutical Fallacies in the Guidelines Established at the (So-Called) 'Conference on Gender-Related Language in Scripture'" (paper presented at the forty-ninth annual meeting of the Evangelical Theological Society, Santa Clara, Calif., November 20–22, 1997), 5.

9. The NIV (not NIVI!) has already chosen to render this "are the feet of *those* who bring good news."

10. Grudem, "What's Wrong," 4.

11. Ibid.

12. Grudem, "What's Wrong" (1996 edition), 6.

13. Ibid. (1997 edition), 5.

14. This particular example is from Strauss, "Guidelines," 10.

15. Trying to handle that pesky gender-specific English pronoun, the NIVI opts for "Surely you will reward everyone [*ʾîsh*] according to what they have done."

16. J. H. Stek, "A Study in the Language of Old Testament Wisdom Literature with Special Focus on Gender Concerns," kindly sent to me by the author in December 1997.

17. So also A.9—but I shall return to that one in chapter 8.

18. Walter Bauer, William F. Arndt, F. Wilbur Gingrich, and Frederick W. Danker, *A Greek-English Lexicon of the New Testament and Other Early Christian Literature* (Chicago: University of Chicago Press, 1979).

19. The argument advanced by some—that this is an instance of a *representative* male, yet still a male—is not compelling. For even if it were right (and I do not think it is), it would not address the problem that the English receptor word may not enjoy the same representative status. We cannot so easily escape the problem of differing semantic ranges.

20. Andreas J. Köstenberger, "The Neutering of 'Man' in the NIVI," *CBMW News* 2.3 (June 1997), 8–13, esp. p. 9.

21. For example, on a related topic, the book Dr. Andreas Köstenberger coauthored with Thomas R. Schreiner and H. Scott Baldwin, *Women in the Church: A Fresh Analysis of 1 Timothy 2:9–15* (Grand Rapids: Baker, 1995), is the most technically competent study of this passage now available.

22. Moreover, we have since discussed the matter personally.

23. Köstenberger, "Neutering," 10.

24. Strauss ("Guidelines," 6) shrewdly observes that when this passage is discussed by Dr. Wayne Grudem in his influential *Systematic Theology* ([Grand Rapids: Zondervan, 1994], 541), it is under the heading "The Humanity of Christ."

25. Elsewhere a slightly different case has been put forward for the preservation of "men . . . man" in this instance. Some scholars take this passage to hint at "new Adam Christology" and therefore want some way to preserve "man/Adam" in the English translation. Whether or not "new Adam Christology" is in view here I shall not dispute. Yet the fact remains that this text is written in Greek, not Hebrew, and the word at issue is Greek *anthrōpos,* not Hebrew *ʾādām.* When the LXX thinks of *ʾādām* as a name, it transliterates it; when as a reference to a human being or to human beings, it translates it into some form of *anthrōpos.* If some translator felt strongly about the need to make a connection between 1 Timothy 2:5 and "new Adam Christology," doubtless he or she could include an explanatory note. But as to the *meaning* of the Greek, the NIVI has it right. I shall return to the confusion between translation and transliteration in chapter 8.

26. I am grateful to Dr. Ronald Youngblood for the documentation. Strauss ("Guidelines," 3) has picked up on this same point.

27. In a private communication as well as in his unpublished paper ("A Response to Mark L. Strauss' Evaluation of the Colorado Springs Translation Guidelines," 5–8), Dr. Wayne Grudem insists that the framers of the CSG meant by "or human beings in general" nothing more than "or gen-

eral human nature," or the like. The phrase was dropped because it was constantly being misunderstood and was not (as Dr. Grudem avers) well worded. Of course, I accept his explanation, but I have retained my brief discussion above because most readers do not have access to such private communication, and one must wrestle with what published documents actually say. Moreover, I would like to think my linguistic clarifications may be useful to some.

28. The NIVI contracts the two clauses: "No foot of people or animals will pass through it." This contraction eliminates the possibility of using "human" as an adjective: "no human foot of animals will pass through it" obviously will not fly. The NIVI is not semantically wrong, but loses the sonorous quality of the repeated clause for no semantic clarity or other gain.

29. Strauss, "Guidelines," 16. That different words do have the same meaning in particular contexts should not come as a surprise. This does not mean that the total semantic range of one word has the total semantic range of another word. But to argue that the two words must therefore be translated differently in specific contexts is to fall once again into "illegitimate totality transfer," briefly discussed in chapter 3 under "Context and Contexts."

30. See Wayne Grudem, "NIV Controversy: Participants Sign Landmark Agreement," *CBMW News* 2.3 (June 1997), 5.

31. Ibid.

32. Once again, there is another Greek word for "parents," namely, *goneis*. But it does not follow that if a New Testament writer had wanted to say "parents" and not "fathers," the language would require that *goneis* be used. In certain contexts, *goneis* and *pateres,* I am arguing, hold the same semantic turf.

Chapter 6: Some Old Testament Passages

1. J. H. Stek, "A Study in the Language of the Regulative *Toroth* of the Pentateuch with Special Focus on Gender Concerns," sent me by the author in December 1997.

2. Ibid., 2.

3. Ibid., 3.

4. For the history, see chapter 1 under "The Current Crisis."

5. John Piper, "Problems in Gender Changes" (document prepared by Dr. John Piper with help from Dr. Wayne Grudem and presented to the group that met in Colorado Springs on May 27, 1997), 7.

6. Ibid., 3.

7. Wayne Grudem, "What's Wrong with Gender-Neutral Bible Translations?" (Libertyville, Ill.: CBMW, 1996), 6.

8. Certainly the Lord Jesus thought that the superscriptions to the Psalms gave historically reliable information: see Matt. 22:41–46, where the validity of Jesus' argument *depends* on that assumption.

9. Wayne Grudem, "Comparing the Two NIVs," *World* 12.5 (April 19, 1997), 15.

10. Grudem, "What's Wrong" (first [1996] edition), 5.

Chapter 7: *Some New Testament Passages*

1. John Piper, "Problems in Gender Changes" (document prepared by Dr. John Piper with help from Dr. Wayne Grudem and presented to the group that met in Colorado Springs on May 27, 1997), 5.

2. Incidentally, *after* writing the sentence bearing this note number, I noticed that I had used the pronoun "you" three times without for a moment supposing that I was restricting the reference to you, gentle reader.

3. Piper, "Problems," 9.

4. Ibid., 4.

5. Ibid., 7–8.

6. Ibid., 5.

7. Some defenders of gender-inclusive Bible translations have charged the NIVI's critics here with misunderstanding Revelation 3:20. In the context, the "door" on which the exalted Jesus is knocking is not the door of the individual's heart, but the door of the church at Laodicea—and therefore, they conclude, this concern for an emphasis on the individual is doubly misplaced. But although the observation about the door is correct, that is, Jesus is knocking at the closed door of a proud church content with her sinful self-sufficiency, nevertheless as in several of the letters to the seven churches, Jesus, while addressing the whole church, commands and invites its members to obedient faith even if the church as a whole does not follow. But this obvious pattern is surely as protected by the NIVI as by the NIV.

8. Wayne Grudem, "Comparing the Two NIVs," *World* 12.5 (April 19, 1997), 16.

9. For example, after the loss of "thou," a sudden shift from second-person singular to second-person plural may be marked by a change from "you" to "you people" as in John 3:11 NIV.

10. Strictly speaking, of course, this is the terminology Jesus used *as John reports him.* Jesus himself may well have been using Aramaic, not Greek, for this exchange.

11. Andreas J. Köstenberger, "The Neutering of 'Man' in the NIVI," *CBMW News* 2.3 (June 1997), 6–7.

12. Grudem, "Comparing," 17.

13. Wayne Grudem, "What's Wrong with Gender-Neutral Bible Translations?" (Libertyville, Ill.: CBMW, 1997), 9–10.

14. I doubt that the "but" is justified here either, but that is another question. At least the NIVI has in my view properly understood *anēr.*

15. Köstenberger, "Neutering," throughout.

16. John R. Kohlenberger III, "Understanding the Current Controversy over Bible Translations" (paper presented at the international convention of the Christian Booksellers Association, Atlanta, Ga., July 14, 1997), under the heading "Translation of the Words for 'Man.'" A slightly edited

version of this paper is available online at http://www.worldstar
.com/~jrk3/inclusive.htm.

Chapter 8: *Some Critical Passages with Important Doctrinal Issues at Stake*

1. The NIV here includes a footnote: "Hebrew *adam.*"

2. The NIVI here includes a footnote: "Hebrew *adam,* traditionally *man.*"

3. Wayne Grudem, "What's Wrong with Gender-Neutral Bible Translations?" (Libertyville, Ill.: CBMW, 1997), 7.

4. Most recently and competently, see Richard S. Hess, "Splitting the Adam," in *Studies in the Pentateuch,* ed. J. A. Emerton, Supplements to Vetus Testamentum 42 (Leiden: E. J. Brill, 1990), 1–15.

5. I am grateful to John H. Stek for reminding me of this obvious fact in an unpublished paper, "Did God 'Call Them *Man*'?" (sent to me by the author in December 1997), 3.

6. For example, Gen. 11:5; Ps. 12:1, 8; 31:19; 145:12; Eccles. 1:13; 2:3; 3:10; Jer. 50:40.

7. Ps. 21:10; 33:13; Prov. 8:31; Dan. 2:28; Joel 1:12. Both the NIV and NIVI normally retain "son of man" in poetic passages when it is in parallel to "man," so as to preserve interesting poetical synonymy rather than collapse them into identical expressions.

8. D. A. Carson, "New Bible Translations: An Assessment and Prospect," in *The Bible in the Twenty-First Century,* ed. Howard Clark Kee (Philadelphia: Trinity Press International, 1993), 56–57.

9. Ibid., 57.

10. That is why the CBT includes Calvinists and Arminians, Baptists and Paedo-Baptists, and so forth.

11. Grudem, "What's Wrong," 8.

12. My assumption is that John 19:36 is indeed referring to Psalm 34. Some scholars draw other connections.

13. John Piper, "Problems in Gender Changes" (document prepared by Dr. John Piper with help from Dr. Wayne Grudem and presented to the group that met in Colorado Springs on May 27, 1997), 7.

14. The NIVI offers a footnote: "Or *what is a human being that you are mindful of him, / the son of man that you care for him?*" and continues to footnote masculine singular alternatives for the plural pronouns in verses 5–6.

15. The NIVI includes a footnote: "Or *What are mere mortals that you are mindful of them, human beings that you care for them? / You made them a little lower than the angels; you crowned them with glory and honour and put everything under their feet.* Psalm 8:4–6."

16. Piper, "Problems," 6.

Chapter 9: *But Is the English Language Changing?*

1. Wayne Grudem, "What's Wrong with Gender-Neutral Bible Translations?" (Libertyville, Ill.: CBMW, 1997), 18–23.

2. D. F. Wright, *Evangelicals Now* 12.9 (September 1997), 17.

3. Dennis E. Baron, *Grammar and Gender* (New Haven: Yale University Press, 1986), 191–97. All of the sources briefly cited in the lines that follow are documented in Baron. Here I provide only the name of the author and the date of the publication, occasionally adding the title.

4. Ibid., 193.

5. Ibid., 195.

6. See especially Jean Aitchison, *Language Change: Progress or Decay?* 2d ed., Cambridge Approaches to Linguistics (Cambridge: Cambridge University Press, 1991); James Milroy, *Linguistic Variation and Change: On the Historical Sociolinguistics of English,* Language in Society 17 (Oxford: Blackwell, 1992); April M. S. McMahon, *Understanding Language Change* (Cambridge: Cambridge University Press, 1994).

7. See especially Christopher R. Seitz, *Word without End: The Old Testament, an Abiding Theological Witness* (Grand Rapids: Eerdmans, 1998), especially chapter 20, "Reader Competence and the Offense of Biblical Language: The Limitations of So-Called Inclusive Language," 292–99.

8. Carl Sagan, *Billions and Billions: Thoughts on Life and Death at the Brink of the Millennium* (New York: Random House, 1997).

9. Oxford: Blackwell, 1996.

10. Ibid., 83.

11. Grand Rapids: Eerdmans, 1995.

12. Ibid., 56.

13. I think those were the exact words. I definitely heard "humankind's"; the rest may not be quite right, for I was in heavy traffic at the time and could not get it down before memory failed.

14. *Time* 151.7 (February 23, 1998), 8.

GENERAL INDEX

Adam, 151, 166–70
Aitchison, Jean, 211
American Standard Version (ASV), 19, 20, 73

Bain, Alexander, 186
Baldwin, H. Scott, 207
Barker, Kenneth L., 32–34, 38, 157, 200
Baron, Dennis E., 185–86, 204–5, 211
Bayly, Tim, 33
Beekman, John, 55, 202
Beitzel, Barry, 202
Bible League, 36
Bilezikian, Gilbert, 30
Bruce, F. F., 202

Callow, John, 55, 202
Carlton, Lillian E., 185
Christianity Today, 35–36
Christians for Biblical Equality, 36
Colorado Springs Guidelines (CSG), 33, 36, 39–40, 44–46, 111–33, 196, 201, 207–8
  aphoristic or universal statements using man or masculine pronouns, 143–44, 149
  brother(s) and sister(s) in place of brother(s), 25, 45, 130–31, 156
  changes in voice (active to passive), 141–42
  child/children instead of son(s), 19, 45–46, 131–33, 176
  generic use of the pronoun, 111–15, 116, 136, 157–58, 184, 186, 189–90
  humankind or human being(s) in place of man, 45, 120–28, 130,

139, 141, 148, 150–51, 153, 158–62, 166–70
  indefinite pronouns, 45, 128–30
  Jesus' humanity or masculinity, 126–27, 150–51, 165, 179–81
  parent(s) or ancestor(s) in place of father(s), 46, 133
  substantival participles, 44, 112, 114
  third-person masculine singular pronouns changed to plural pronouns, 20, 23, 38, 45, 105–8, 116, 135–38, 140, 149, 152, 154–55, 157, 160
  third-person masculine singular pronouns changed to second-person pronouns, 43, 118–120
  See also Committee on Bible Translation, translation guidelines
Colorado Springs meeting, 33–35, 40, 147, 184
Committee on Bible Translation (CBT), 29, 162, 199
  members of, 16, 26, 28, 32, 197, 210
  purpose for, 26, 145, 191
  translation guidelines, 37, 39–40, 41–44, 100–111, 144, 194, 201, 205
    contextual particularity (or contextual specificity). *See* translation theory, guidelines for translators
    historical particularity (or historical specificity). *See* translation theory, guidelines for translators
    intracanonical connections and the preserving of form. *See* translation theory, guidelines for translators
    male-specified professions

213

Scripture Index